AI Capitalism: The Last 5 Years Of Labor
By: Patrice Shabazz

This is a work of [fiction/nonfiction]. Names, characters, places, and incidents are the product of the author's imagination or are used in a transformative and educational context. Any resemblance to actual persons, living or dead, or actual events is purely coincidental unless otherwise noted.

For permission requests, contact:
Patrice Shabazz
Email: patriceshabazz39@gmail.com
Publisher: Exclusive Heights

ISBN: 978-1-969629-74-7
First Edition: 2025

Cover art by Patrice Shabazz
Printed in the United States of America

Chapter 1: The American Dream Was Always a Lease

Prophecy Opener

They sold the American Dream as a promise of permanence: white picket fences, two-car garages, manicured lawns, and a key that meant freedom. But the truth has always been uglier, buried beneath slogans and mortgage paperwork. The dream wasn't built for ownership — it was built for debt. It was designed as a lease with the bank, the state, and the system as landlords.

The so-called dream is not about possession. It is about participation in a cycle where every paycheck, every tax, every late fee, every property reassessment feeds the machine.

The prophecy is this: in an age of AI and automation, the dream will not dissolve. It will tighten. Shelter will become subscription. Cars will be leased from fleets you never own. Furniture, software, even appliances will be locked behind recurring payments. The house you think is yours will belong to the bank until the day you die.

The American Dream was never ownership. It was a contract of captivity disguised as aspiration.

Psychological Breakdown

Debt as Identity

People confuse debt with achievement. A mortgage is celebrated as proof of success, but it is a shackle that guarantees decades of labor to service it. Pride becomes a leash.

Fear of Losing Shelter

Housing is weaponized. Families will endure exploitation at work or silence injustices in fear of foreclosure or eviction. The system uses fear of homelessness as silent obedience training.

Illusion of Stability

The dream markets itself as security, but property taxes, maintenance costs, insurance, and interest ensure instability. Homeowners live one emergency away from collapse.

Shame of Failure

Foreclosure is framed as personal weakness rather than systemic robbery. Families internalize guilt, protecting the illusion while hiding their scars.

Generational Trauma

Children raised in unstable housing conditions inherit anxiety, distrust, and often debt themselves. The dream becomes a curse passed down.

Case Studies / Real-Life Examples

Case Study 1: Post-War Housing Boom

After WWII, the GI Bill helped millions of white veterans buy homes, but Black veterans were systematically denied. The dream was racially gated. Ownership was access, but only for some.

Case Study 2: Redlining

Banks drew red lines on maps, refusing loans to minority communities. Families inside those zones were forced to rent indefinitely, while others built generational equity. Housing was a tool of segregation.

Case Study 3: Subprime Crisis of 2008

Predatory loans, ballooning interest rates, and bundled mortgage securities created a bubble. When it burst, millions lost homes. Banks were bailed out. Families were evicted. The dream revealed itself as profit machinery, not protection.

Case Study 4: Modern Rent Crisis

Rents rise faster than wages in nearly every major city. Housing is not built for tenants to thrive, but to extract maximum rent for landlords and investors.

Case Study 5: Corporate Landlords

Today, hedge funds buy foreclosed homes in bulk and rent them back to the public. Families who once dreamed of ownership are reduced to tenants in houses their parents built.

Corporate vs. Street POV

Corporate: "A mortgage is ownership."
Street: "A mortgage is a 30-year rental with paperwork."

Corporate: "Home values prove prosperity."
Street: "Values rise so landlords can push you out."

Corporate: "Renting is throwing money away."
Street: "So is paying interest to a bank forever."

Corporate: "Property taxes support communities."
Street: "They guarantee you'll never stop paying for the house you 'own.'"

Parable

Marcus grew up believing a house was freedom. At twenty-eight, he took out a mortgage for a modest home, working double shifts to pay. For ten years he labored, convinced he was securing his family's future. Then a layoff hit, the bills piled, and the bank repossessed. Marcus realized too late that he never truly owned the home — he was leasing it from a system that sold him the illusion of permanence. The key in his pocket had never been his.

Story with a Lesson

In the 1980s, a Black family in Chicago fought for a mortgage after being denied repeatedly. They finally purchased through a "contract for deed," a predatory agreement that looked like ownership but wasn't. For years they paid faithfully, but when repairs mounted and payments ballooned, they lost everything. That family, like thousands of others, learned the hidden lesson: ownership is conditional. The paperwork may say buyer, but the system treats you as tenant until the debt is cleared — and even then, taxes mean you can still lose it.

Chapter Manifesto

We declare: the American Dream is a lie sold as a lease.

We reject the story that mortgages equal ownership. We reject the theft of generational wealth through predatory loans, taxes, and foreclosure. We reject the lie that rent is weakness while debt is strength.

Our manifesto: shelter is a right, not a chain. Homes must be liberated from banks, not bound to them. True ownership means independence from perpetual debt.

Survival Solutions

Community Land Trusts
Communities pooling resources to own land collectively, shielding it from speculative markets.

Tenant Unions
Renters organizing to resist predatory landlords, demand repairs, and freeze unjust rent hikes.

Debt Resistance
Movements that refuse predatory payments, exposing fraud and demanding renegotiation.

Alternative Housing Models
Tiny homes, off-grid building, and cooperative living that bypass banks and developers.

Generational Planning
Families teaching children the truth of mortgages, preparing them to build outside traditional debt traps.

Future Scenario

By 2040, housing will be dominated by corporate ownership. Families will not buy homes outright but subscribe to "living packages" — monthly fees for shelter, utilities, and maintenance bundled. Smart locks will enforce evictions remotely. Banks and hedge funds will own entire neighborhoods.

But resistance will rise. Communities will occupy abandoned properties, creating sovereign neighborhoods outside the system. Underground housing economies will flourish, where families barter labor for shelter, bypassing banks.

Prophecy Close & Lesson

The American Dream was not stolen — it was never real. It was scripted to keep families working, paying, and hoping for freedom that never comes.

The lesson is this: you cannot own freedom on credit. Debt is not ownership. A house does not equal liberation when it comes with chains. Until we reclaim shelter as a right, the dream will remain a lease.

Chapter 2: Jobs Are Not Security, They're Shackles

Prophecy Opener

They told you to "get a good job." They told you loyalty would be rewarded, pensions would keep you safe, and promotions would mark your rise. But jobs were never security. They were contracts of control. They were shackles dressed up as ladders.

The paycheck looks like freedom, but it's engineered dependence. The benefits look like protection, but they're designed as handcuffs. The boss looks like leadership, but they're middle-management guards in the prison of wage labor.

The prophecy is this: as automation rises, jobs will not become safer or more stable — they will become more fragile. Layoffs will come not from managers but from algorithms. Shifts will vanish without explanation. The promise of security will collapse into proof of captivity. In the machine age, work itself will reveal what it always was: survival rent.

Psychological Breakdown

The Illusion of Loyalty

Workers are told companies are families. But when profit margins drop, families don't fire their children. Loyalty is one-sided — employees sacrifice, corporations replace.

Fear as Motivation

Fear of losing health insurance, rent money, or retirement funds keeps workers obedient. Fear is the leash that guarantees compliance.

Identity Fusion

People define themselves by their jobs: "I'm a teacher," "I'm a machinist," "I'm a nurse." When layoffs come, identity collapses, leaving trauma beyond financial ruin.

Shame of Job Loss

Society frames unemployment as personal failure rather than systemic design. Workers internalize guilt, shielding corporations from blame.

The Retirement Mirage

The system teaches that jobs equal security if you endure long enough. But pensions have been stripped, Social Security weakened, and "golden years" deferred into extinction.

Case Studies / Real-Life Examples

Case Study 1: Company Towns

Mining towns once paid wages in scrip redeemable only at company stores. Jobs secured survival only by deepening dependence. Workers never escaped debt.

Case Study 2: The Rust Belt Collapse

Factories in Detroit, Cleveland, and Pittsburgh promised lifelong stability. Automation and outsourcing erased millions of jobs, leaving ghost towns where "security" once stood.

Case Study 3: Modern Gig Work

Uber and Amazon Flex workers are told they are "independent." But without benefits, protections, or stability, they live under constant precarity — shackled to platforms instead of employers.

Case Study 4: COVID-19 Layoffs

In 2020, millions were deemed "essential" and then discarded weeks later. Security evaporated overnight, exposing jobs as transactional, not protective.

Case Study 5: The Middle Management Trap

White-collar jobs, once symbols of status, now face the same instability as factory work. Layoffs arrive by email. Security is an illusion across every class.

Corporate vs. Street POV

Corporate: "Jobs create stability."
Street: "Jobs create dependency."

Corporate: "Work hard, and you'll rise."
Street: "Work hard, and you'll burn out while the boss cashes in."

Corporate: "We're a family here."
Street: "Families don't replace you with software."

Corporate: "Your benefits keep you safe."
Street: "Your benefits are chains — they keep you from leaving."

Parable

Terrell worked twenty-five years at the same shipping company. He never missed a shift, trained dozens of new hires, and believed he had earned loyalty. When automation arrived, a machine replaced him. His severance was a handshake and a pamphlet about "new opportunities." Terrell realized too late: his decades of service were not security. They were decades of shackles polished with false promises.

Story with a Lesson

In the 1930s, sharecroppers in the South were told jobs on plantations meant survival. They were given land, seed, and shelter but kept in endless cycles of debt. Each season, wages vanished into fees and charges. Their labor sustained the landowners while their families remained impoverished. This is the blueprint modern jobs still follow: laborers are promised stability, but the system is designed so survival requires constant work. Jobs are the new sharecropping — only the crops are hours, and the landowner is the corporation.

Chapter Manifesto

We declare: jobs are not security. They are shackles.

We reject the illusion that loyalty earns protection. We reject the guilt imposed on workers when corporations betray them. We reject the myth that survival must be leased through wages.

Our manifesto: security must be built outside the leash of jobs. True survival cannot come from dependency on systems designed to discard.

Survival Solutions

Side Hustle Sovereignty

Build independent streams of income that corporations cannot revoke.

Skill Ownership

Invest in skills transferable outside traditional jobs: trades, technology, agriculture, community organizing.

Cooperative Labor Models

Form worker-owned businesses where profit circulates among members rather than siphoning upward.

Emergency Funds and Exit Plans

Prioritize financial independence, even in small amounts, to avoid total collapse when layoffs come.

Union Revitalization

Where possible, fight for collective bargaining to resist arbitrary firings and secure worker rights.

Future Scenario

By 2035, jobs as we know them will be largely gone. AI scheduling systems will assign shifts by algorithm, treating humans as disposable cogs. Benefits will disappear into gig-style contracts. Workers will rotate between short-term roles with no stability.

But in the margins, new models will rise. Worker co-ops, sovereign communities, and independent hustlers will survive outside corporate chains. Those who build outside dependence will thrive.

Prophecy Close & Lesson

Jobs were never ladders. They were always leashes. They were marketed as protection but designed as prisons.

The lesson is this: you cannot build freedom on the foundation of dependency. To break the shackles, survival must be claimed beyond the paycheck.

Chapter 3: The Middle Class Illusion

Prophecy Opener

They told you the middle class was proof that America worked. They said if you studied hard, followed rules, and stayed loyal to the system, you'd rise above struggle into comfort. A house in the suburbs. Two cars in the driveway. College funds for the kids. Vacations every summer. Safety.

But the middle class was never security — it was a mirage. A stage set, painted for belief, designed to make the working poor think upward mobility was possible. The middle class was a leash, not a ladder. A temporary holding cell between poverty and wealth, destined to collapse when the math no longer worked.

The prophecy is this: the middle class will not survive automation, inflation, and debt traps. What once looked like stability will dissolve into either struggle or elite capture. The middle will vanish, leaving only the top and the bottom — masters and servants, owners and renters, programmers and programmed.

Psychological Breakdown

The Comfort Drug

The middle class is designed to make people feel safe enough not to revolt but pressured enough to keep working. Mortgages, car payments, and tuition costs keep them chained to jobs they hate.

Identity Investment

The middle class ties identity to lifestyle — the house, the cars, the vacations. Losing any piece feels like failure, even when the game itself is rigged.

Shame Spiral

When people slide down from the middle class, they're told it's personal mismanagement, not systemic failure. Shame isolates them, keeping them silent instead of rebelling.

Generational Burden

Parents teach children to chase the same illusions — "Go to school, get a good job, buy a house" — even as those promises collapse. The cycle repeats as generational debt.

Illusion of Choice

The middle class feels free because they can pick between brands, neighborhoods, and schools. But the big decisions — land ownership, corporate wealth, policy — are out of their hands.

Case Studies / Real-Life Examples

Case Study 1: The GI Bill Boom

After WWII, veterans were offered housing loans and education benefits. This birthed the suburban middle class — but it excluded many Black veterans, showing how the illusion was selectively granted.

Case Study 2: The 2008 Housing Crash

Millions of middle-class families lost homes when the mortgage system collapsed. Security evaporated overnight, exposing the fragility of "ownership."

Case Study 3: Student Debt Crisis

College degrees were sold as the ticket to middle-class stability. Instead, they chained millions with debt while wages stagnated. The illusion of advancement became a lifetime of repayment.

Case Study 4: The Disappearing Pension

Retirement plans that once guaranteed stability were gutted, replaced with 401(k)s vulnerable to market swings. Security became speculation.

Case Study 5: Inflation and Stagnant Wages

While living costs rise, wages for middle-class jobs have barely moved in decades. What once bought comfort now buys survival.

Corporate vs. Street POV

Corporate: “The middle class is the backbone of America.”

Street: “The middle class is the cushion that keeps the poor from colliding with the rich.”

Corporate: “Work hard and you’ll join the middle class.”

Street: “Work hard and you’ll buy a cage with a mortgage and call it freedom.”

Corporate: “The system rewards responsibility.”

Street: “The system rewards obedience until it doesn’t need you anymore.”

Parable

A man named Carlos saved every penny, worked overtime, and bought a three-bedroom house. For ten years, he felt secure. Then his company outsourced jobs overseas.

He lost his paycheck, but the mortgage stayed the same. Within months, his dream collapsed into foreclosure. The neighbors whispered about his "bad luck." Carlos realized too late: his security was never real. It was borrowed time.

Story with a Lesson

During the rise of the auto industry, Detroit promised the middle class dream — stable jobs, pensions, homes. Workers believed they had cracked the code of American stability. But when factories closed and automation replaced hands, whole communities collapsed into poverty. The lesson: the middle class was not a permanent class. It was a holding pattern, dependent on economic conditions that could change in an instant.

Chapter Manifesto

We declare: the middle class was a stage, not a foundation.

We reject the illusion that comfort equals freedom. We reject the shame imposed on families who slide down when the system collapses. We reject the lie that middle-class life is the reward for hard work, when it is really the bait for compliance.

Our manifesto: survival requires breaking the illusion and building outside the staged ladder.

Survival Solutions

Downsize with Purpose

Reject the pressure to live the middle-class lifestyle as proof of success. Cut unnecessary debt and focus on sovereignty, not image.

Community Pooling

Build neighborhood cooperatives for childcare, schooling, and food to lower dependence on corporate systems.

Ownership in Assets, Not Image

Invest in land, businesses, and intellectual property rather than houses and cars meant for appearances.

Financial Literacy and Resistance

Teach the next generation that survival is not about climbing into the middle, but about building outside it.

Reject Lifestyle Inflation

More income should not mean more debt. Direct surplus into freedom tools — emergency funds, investments, ownership.

Future Scenario

By 2040, the middle class will be extinct. The "middle" will exist only in marketing slogans. Most families will be pushed into renter status, working multiple jobs while paying landlords and corporations for survival. Those who cling to the illusion will drown in debt.

But in the ruins, some will carve new models — sovereign communities, digital hustlers, creators, and cooperatives. They will reject the illusion and build tribes outside the staged show.

Prophecy Close & Lesson

The middle class was never meant to last. It was a curtain painted to keep people performing. The illusion is collapsing, and those who cling to it will fall with it.

The lesson is this: you cannot survive by chasing the middle. Survival comes only by building outside the illusion, by rejecting comfort as captivity and creating systems that are truly ours.

Chapter 4: The School-to-Job Pipeline

Prophecy Opener

They told you education was the golden key. “Stay in school,” they said, “and you’ll unlock success.” They told you the diploma was the passport out of poverty, the bridge into the middle class, the guarantee of a job. But the truth was hidden in the fine print: school wasn’t built to free you. It was built to train you — to shape obedient workers, not liberated thinkers.

From the first bell to the last exam, the school-to-job pipeline is a conveyor belt. It doesn’t prepare children to own, it prepares them to serve. It doesn’t teach sovereignty, it teaches compliance. The prophecy is this: as AI dismantles the job market, the entire purpose of schooling — to funnel bodies into labor — will be exposed as a scam. The pipeline will still exist, but instead of leading to jobs, it will lead to debt, disillusionment, and despair.

Psychological Breakdown

Obedience Training

Schools condition children to follow schedules, obey authority, and measure self-worth by grades. It is less about knowledge and more about compliance.

Creativity Suppression

Art, music, and critical thinking are cut first. Innovation is discouraged because it produces rebels, not workers.

Credential Addiction

Children are told their value depends on degrees, not skills or vision. They become addicted to external validation.

Debt Conditioning

The school pipeline trains people to accept debt early — student loans are framed as "investments," normalizing lifelong financial bondage.

Dream Deferral

By the time most graduate, they have been told to lower expectations, to accept stability over passion, survival over sovereignty.

Case Studies / Real-Life Examples

Case Study 1: The Factory Model of Education

Prussian schools in the 19th century were designed to produce soldiers and workers for industry. America copied this model, turning schools into factories for human capital.

Case Study 2: The Student Loan Crisis

Over $1.7 trillion in U.S. student debt shows how the pipeline funnels young people into financial captivity before they ever start life.

Case Study 3: Job Market Disconnect

Graduates flood into fields with no demand, while trades and ownership skills go untaught. The pipeline doesn't match reality — it produces followers, not leaders.

Case Study 4: Corporate Influence

Textbooks and curriculums are often influenced by corporate donors, ensuring that students learn consumer loyalty rather than independence.

Case Study 5: AI Exposing the Lie

As automation replaces jobs, the myth of education guaranteeing security is unraveling. Degrees are becoming overpriced tickets to nowhere.

Corporate vs. Street POV

Corporate: "Education is the path to success."
Street: "Education is the path to debt and dependency unless you flip the script."

Corporate: "Stay in school and get a good job."
Street: "Stay in school and learn how to beg for a paycheck instead of building your own."

Corporate: "The diploma is proof of your value."
Street: "The diploma is proof you played the game, not that you own the rules."

Parable

A boy named Tyrone loved fixing bikes. He could take apart chains, wheels, gears, and put them back better than new. But his teachers told him bikes wouldn't pay the bills. They pushed him to college. He took out loans, majored in business, and graduated with debt but no job. Meanwhile, his old neighbor opened a bike repair shop, expanded into e-bikes, and built wealth. Tyrone had the passion but was told to ignore it. The pipeline stole his power.

Story with a Lesson

In the 1980s, America's schools pushed "college for all" as the golden rule. Kids were told trades and hustles were beneath them. By the 2000s, electricians, plumbers, and welders were making six figures, while college grads were drowning in debt and working retail. The system wasn't broken — it worked exactly as designed: funnel bodies into debt, strip communities of practical skills, and leave people chasing jobs that don't exist.

Chapter Manifesto

We declare: education is not freedom when it is chained to debt, obedience, and false promises.

We reject the lie that diplomas equal destiny. We reject the conditioning that trains children to follow instead of create. We reject the idea that school prepares people for life when it only prepares them for labor.

Our manifesto: true education is ownership education. True learning builds sovereignty, not servitude.

Survival Solutions

Teach Outside the System

Families and communities must pass down financial literacy, trades, and ownership skills — knowledge schools refuse to teach.

Reject Credential Worship

Skills, creativity, and execution matter more than diplomas. Stop measuring value by degrees.

Early Ownership Training

Teach youth to create businesses, art, and products before they ever enter the debt pipeline.

Debt Resistance

Reject unnecessary student loans. Build careers through apprenticeships, self-study, and entrepreneurship.

Community Schools

Build alternative education spaces focused on sovereignty — coding collectives, trade schools, storytelling hubs.

Future Scenario

By 2040, the school-to-job pipeline will be exposed as an obsolete system. AI will teach faster than human teachers, and corporate influence will grow even stronger. Traditional diplomas will lose value, but debt will remain.

In its place, sovereign education will rise — communities teaching their own, tribes training survival skills, and independent creators building schools outside the corporate model. Children will either be owned by the pipeline or freed by new systems. The choice will be urgent.

Prophecy Close & Lesson

The school-to-job pipeline was never about freedom — it was about supply chains for labor.

The prophecy closes with this: the conveyor belt is breaking. The diplomas will not save you. The only education worth having is the kind that teaches you to own, build, and resist. If we do not reclaim learning, the next generation will graduate not into jobs, but into captivity.

Chapter 5: The Myth of Retirement

Prophecy Opener

They told you to keep working, keep saving, keep trusting. They promised one day you would sit back in a rocking chair, sip sweet tea on the porch, and live out your golden years in peace. “Work hard and your reward is rest,” they said. But retirement was never meant to free you. It was meant to keep you believing.

The prophecy is this: in a system addicted to profit, retirement will collapse. Social Security will shrink. Pensions will evaporate. Savings will be consumed by inflation, medical bills, and market crashes. The dream of retiring at 65 will be replaced by the nightmare of working until death. The golden years will turn into rust.

Psychological Breakdown

Deferred Life Syndrome

People are trained to put off joy, rest, and freedom until retirement. Life becomes a waiting room.

Illusion of Security

Social Security and pensions are framed as guarantees when they are political bargaining chips.

Fear of Poverty

Workers cling to jobs not for meaning, but out of fear of losing the promise of retirement benefits.

Erosion of Dignity

When older workers can’t retire, they compete with younger ones for low-wage jobs, erasing dignity.

Normalization of Endless Labor

The culture shifts so far that “working until you die” becomes admirable, not tragic.

Case Studies / Real-Life Examples

Case Study 1: The Pension Collapse

From steelworkers in the 1980s to teachers in the 2000s, countless pension systems promised security then cut benefits or went bankrupt. Workers spent decades paying into plans that disappeared overnight.

Case Study 2: Social Security’s Strain

An aging population and political attacks threaten to reduce Social Security. By 2035, projections show potential cuts unless drastic changes are made.

Case Study 3: 401(k) Gamble

Instead of guaranteed pensions, workers were pushed into 401(k) plans tied to the stock market. A single crash can wipe out decades of savings.

Case Study 4: Healthcare Drain

Medical bills in old age devour retirement savings faster than any vacation or luxury. Retirement money often goes straight to hospitals and drug companies.

Case Study 5: Japan and America’s Aging Workforce

Japan’s rising elderly workforce mirrors what’s coming to the U.S. Older people working into their 70s and 80s will no longer be an exception — it will be the rule.

Corporate vs. Street POV

Corporate: “Retirement is your reward for hard work.”

Street: “Retirement is the carrot they dangle while they take your life energy.”

Corporate: “Social Security is a safety net.”
Street: “Social Security is a weak leash — they can cut it whenever they want.”

Corporate: “Invest in your 401(k) and you’ll be fine.”
Street: “Your 401(k) is a casino chip — and Wall Street is the house.”

Parable

Ruth worked 40 years at a factory, saving every penny in her pension fund. She dreamed of retiring at 65. But when her company “restructured,” the pension was slashed. Ruth went to Walmart at 68 to work as a greeter just to afford groceries. She told customers, “I thought I’d be free by now.” The system sold her a dream and delivered chains.

Story with a Lesson

In 2008, millions of Americans nearing retirement watched half their savings vanish in a market crash. Some had worked 30–40 years, faithfully contributing to 401(k)s. Overnight, decades of sacrifice disappeared. Many never recovered. The lesson: retirement in this system is not a guarantee — it’s a gamble stacked against you.

Chapter Manifesto

We declare: retirement is not a promise. It is a trap.

We reject the lie that life’s joy must be delayed until old age. We reject the idea that pensions and Social Security are untouchable guarantees. We reject the normalization of endless work as noble.

Our manifesto: life must be lived now. Security must be built outside their systems. Dignity is not waiting to die after 40 years of labor.

Survival Solutions

Ownership Now, Not Later

Invest in businesses, land, and intellectual property that outlast wages. Don't wait for retirement to own.

Community Retirement Systems

Create collective funds and group support models instead of relying solely on government programs.

Health as Wealth

Prioritize health early so medical bills don't consume later years.

Alternative Income Streams

Books, media, small businesses, and investments must supplement or replace fragile retirement accounts.

Live Before Retirement

Reject deferred life syndrome. Take time for freedom and fulfillment before old age.

Future Scenario

By 2050, retirement as we know it will no longer exist. The old promise of "work, save, and rest" will be replaced by "work until death." Entire generations will live paycheck-to-paycheck into their 70s and 80s. Social Security will be rationed, healthcare privatized, and pensions extinct.

But resistance will rise. Communities will create sovereign retirement systems. People will reject waiting until 65 to live, instead building parallel economies where life, joy, and rest exist throughout adulthood. The fight will be to redefine retirement not as the end of life, but as the reclaiming of life — at every age.

Prophecy Close & Lesson

Retirement was never the golden years. It was a golden cage.

The prophecy closes with this: the system never planned to let you rest. The dream of retirement is collapsing, and those who cling to it will collapse too. The only path forward is to own now, build now, live now. The golden years are not promised — they must be created.

Chapter 6: Consumerism — The Distraction That Fed the Beast

Prophecy Opener

They told you that you were free because you could choose what to buy. Freedom was branded, boxed, and shelved. You were told you could define yourself by the clothes on your back, the car you drove, the gadgets in your pocket. They sold you the illusion that ownership of things was ownership of life.

But the prophecy is this: consumerism was never freedom. It was distraction. While you were busy chasing sneakers, screens, and sales, the system built cages around your labor, your time, and your mind. You thought you were eating at the table, but you were the meal. The beast fed on your distraction, and it grew fat while you stayed hungry.

Psychological Breakdown

Identity Substitution

Instead of identity being rooted in essence, family, or values, it is hijacked by brands. People say, "I'm a Nike guy," "I'm an Apple person," as if companies replace tribes.

Endless Desire Loop

Advertising programs dissatisfaction: you are never enough without the next product. Scarcity is manufactured in the mind.

Debt as Normality

Credit cards, loans, and buy-now-pay-later systems normalize being perpetually in debt. Consumerism chains freedom to interest rates.

Peer Pressure Amplification

Culture shifts from need to want. Social validation is built on owning things, not character.

Distraction from Structural Oppression

Consumerism hides systemic inequality by offering shallow victories: “At least you got the new Jordans.”

Case Studies / Real-Life Examples

Case Study 1: Black Friday

Every year, shoppers trample one another for flat-screen TVs and gaming consoles. Violence over discounts shows how consumerism manipulates survival instincts.

Case Study 2: iPhone Culture

Apple turned phones into identity tokens. People go into debt every year to upgrade devices with minimal improvements, driven by status pressure.

Case Study 3: Fast Fashion

Clothing chains churn out disposable clothes that collapse after a season. Factories exploit overseas workers while consumers in the West brag about cheap hauls.

Case Study 4: The Subprime Mortgage Crisis

Consumer desire for bigger homes was weaponized through predatory loans. Millions lost houses, proving consumerism was not empowerment — it was bait.

Case Study 5: The Streaming Trap

Endless subscriptions eat away at incomes while distracting from real-world survival. People rent access to joy instead of building it.

Corporate vs. Street POV

Corporate: “Consumer choice is freedom.”
Street: “Choice between brands is still chains — they own both sides.”

Corporate: “We create products people want.”
Street: “You create addictions people can’t escape.”

Corporate: “We empower lifestyles.”
Street: “You sell illusions and steal futures.”

Parable

Marcus loved sneakers. Every drop, every limited edition, he had to have it. He worked double shifts just to keep up. By 35, his closet was worth thousands — but his savings account was empty. When layoffs came, Marcus had shoes he couldn’t eat, boxes he couldn’t trade for rent. The sneakers made him rich in image and broke in reality. Consumerism owned him.

Story with a Lesson

In the 1990s, Nike built campaigns around Michael Jordan that made sneakers into holy relics. Entire communities went broke chasing them. Murders even occurred over pairs of Jordans. Meanwhile, Nike factories paid overseas workers pennies. The lesson: consumerism is not just expensive — it’s bloody. It trades lives for logos.

Chapter Manifesto

We declare: consumerism is not freedom.

We reject the lie that our value is measured by possessions. We reject the normalization of debt as empowerment. We reject the idea that identity can be bought at the mall.

Our manifesto: true wealth is ownership of self, time, and community. Not cars. Not clothes. Not gadgets.

Survival Solutions

Minimalism with Strategy

Live with less, but invest in more — own assets, not endless consumer goods.

Community Sharing Models

Instead of each person drowning in debt, communities can pool resources: shared tools, cars, libraries of goods.

Financial Literacy

Teach children and adults alike how to see through consumer traps.

Rebrand Wealth

Shift status from what you wear to what you own, build, and pass on.

Digital Detox

Step back from ads, influencers, and content designed to manipulate. Starve the beast.

Future Scenario

By 2050, consumerism will become even more invasive. Ads will read your face, your emotions, your biometrics. Products will be personalized traps. Debt will be automated — purchases deducted before you even decide.

The hustle will not be to earn money, but to resist spending it before it leaves your hands.

But there will be resistance. Tribes will reject consumerism. New models of ownership will emerge — land, food systems, intellectual property. People will learn that freedom is not buying, but building.

Prophecy Close & Lesson

The prophecy closes with this: consumerism was not just distraction. It was a leash. Every dollar spent chasing brands was a dollar stolen from sovereignty. The beast fed while people starved. To break free, the people must starve the beast — and feed themselves.

Chapter 7: Why the System Needs You to Stay Sleep

Prophecy Opener

They don't need you awake. They don't want you awake. They built an entire empire on your sleep. Not the kind of sleep that rests the body — the kind that dulls the mind. You wake up at 6 a.m. to punch in, you stay awake long enough to obey, and then you collapse into distraction. They sold you dreams through TV screens, anesthetized you with comfort, numbed you with entertainment.

The prophecy is this: a population asleep is easier to herd than a population awake. As long as you are sleepwalking through debt, distracted by headlines, addicted to phones, and hypnotized by brands, you will never resist. The system's greatest weapon is not violence, but sedation.

Psychological Breakdown

The Comfort Drug

People trade freedom for comfort. As long as the couch is soft, the food is cheap, and the Wi-Fi is on, rebellion feels unnecessary.

Learned Helplessness

Generations are conditioned to believe nothing can change. The individual feels powerless, so he sleeps to escape.

Noise as Numbness

Constant news, music, and media overload people until they shut down thought. The mind drowns in stimulation, not silence.

Fear of Awakening

To wake up is to see the chains — and that brings responsibility. Many prefer the dream because the truth is heavy.

Dependency on Distraction

Phones, sports, and gossip become intravenous drips of sedation. Sleepwalking becomes culture.

Case Studies / Real-Life Examples

Case Study 1: Bread and Circuses

Rome kept its people pacified with games and grain. While gladiators fought, the empire rotted. The people didn't notice until collapse.

Case Study 2: The TV Era

In the 1950s, television became the new babysitter of the masses. Propaganda, commercials, and sitcoms shaped identity and politics while numbing resistance.

Case Study 3: The Smartphone Era

By the 2010s, phones became the modern opiate. Endless scrolling, infinite feeds, and algorithmic manipulation created a nation of digital sleepwalkers.

Case Study 4: The Student Loan Trap

Young people are lulled into debt under the illusion of education, but most never break free. The "dream" of a degree sedates resistance until middle age.

Case Study 5: The Suburban Cocoon

Comfortable homes and malls lulled millions into believing stability was permanent, even as wages collapsed.

Corporate vs. Street POV

Corporate: “We give people entertainment.”
Street: “You drug people with distraction.”

Corporate: “The people are too apathetic to change.”
Street: “The people are sedated on purpose.”

Corporate: “If it ain’t broke, don’t fix it.”
Street: “It’s broken, but you made us too numb to care.”

Parable

Jerome worked two jobs. When he came home, he collapsed on the couch and scrolled TikTok until his eyes burned. He always said, “One day I’ll get out of this.” But the days became years. One night, his daughter asked, “Daddy, why don’t we ever do anything fun?” Jerome realized he had spent a decade sleepwalking. The system never told him to resist — it just rocked him to sleep.

Story with a Lesson

In Nazi Germany, entire towns lived next to concentration camps yet claimed ignorance. Why? Sedation. People chose to stay asleep because waking up meant confronting evil and risking their lives. The lesson: systems thrive when people would rather not know. The same dynamic exists today — atrocities in prisons, sweatshops, and wars go unchallenged because the masses prefer not to wake up.

Chapter Manifesto

We declare: sleep is not safety.

We reject the comfort drug that keeps us numb. We reject the idea that distraction is harmless. We reject the lie that nothing can change.

Our manifesto: awakening is dangerous, but necessary. Comfort is the true cage. To be awake is to fight, to resist, to live.

Survival Solutions

Digital Fasts
Schedule time away from screens to break dependency.

Rebuild Silence
Spend time in thought, meditation, or conversation without media noise.

Truth-Telling Tribes
Form groups where honesty is valued over comfort.

Cut Comfort Addictions
Challenge the culture of endless snacks, streaming, and scrolling. Reclaim discomfort as growth.

Education Outside Institutions
Read radical texts, history, and hidden knowledge the system doesn't teach.

Future Scenario

By 2050, sedation will be biological. Pills, implants, and VR worlds will keep masses pacified while elites extract labor and resources. Whole generations may spend more time in digital dreams than physical reality.

But resistance will rise. Some will unplug. Communities will build sober spaces where waking up is sacred. The battle will not be over wealth or land — it will be over consciousness.

Prophecy Close & Lesson

The prophecy closes with this: the system doesn't fear your strength — it fears your awakening. Sleep is the greatest weapon of control. To resist is to open your eyes, even when the dream is sweeter. Comfort is the drug. Awakening is the cure.

Chapter 8: The Silent Layoff — AI in the Workplace

Prophecy Opener

Pink slips used to come from a boss with a face. Now they arrive as a notification, a login that suddenly doesn't work, a schedule that never reappears. You don't get fired by a human anymore — you get erased by an algorithm. The manager doesn't even know why you're gone. The system simply decided.

The prophecy is this: the age of AI will bring a new kind of layoff. Not loud, not public, not even explained. Silent layoffs, invisible replacements, whole departments vanishing without notice. And the workers will wake up one day to find their jobs replaced by machines that never asked for a paycheck.

Psychological Breakdown

The Invisible Boss
Workers are used to blaming a supervisor. With AI, there's no one to confront, no one to negotiate with. Power becomes faceless.

The Fear of Redundancy
Employees live with a low-grade paranoia: "Will I be next?" The uncertainty becomes a form of control.

The Erosion of Dignity
Being replaced by another human at least acknowledged skill. Being replaced by code tells you your humanity has no value.

Gaslighting by Optimism

Companies tell workers, "AI is here to help you," even as it replaces them. The dissonance paralyzes resistance.

The Loneliness of Displacement

Silent layoffs mean no closure, no union action, no headlines — just disappearance. Workers lose even the solidarity of shared struggle.

Case Studies / Real-Life Examples

Case Study 1: The Call Center Collapse

AI chatbots now handle millions of customer service calls. Entire overseas call centers were shut down with little warning. Workers simply logged in and found no shifts.

Case Study 2: Warehouse Robots

Amazon quietly replaced thousands of pickers with robotic arms and conveyor algorithms. Human workers weren't fired all at once — their hours were simply cut until they quit.

Case Study 3: Journalism and AI Writing

Local newspapers in the U.S. replaced reporters with AI-generated articles for sports and finance. Writers were told they were "transitioning" into new roles, but most were laid off within a year.

Case Study 4: The Fast-Food Kiosk

Chains like McDonald's and Taco Bell introduced ordering kiosks, reducing cashier roles. Employees were never "fired" — they just weren't scheduled.

Case Study 5: The IT Department Downsizing

AI-driven network monitoring tools quietly eliminated entire teams. The announcement wasn't "You're fired," but "We no longer require manual oversight."

Corporate vs. Street POV

Corporate: "AI makes work more efficient."
Street: "AI makes workers disposable."

Corporate: "Automation frees humans for more creative work."
Street: "Automation frees corporations from paying humans at all."

Corporate: "No one is losing jobs, they're evolving."
Street: "Jobs don't evolve — they evaporate."

Parable

Tasha worked at a logistics company for 12 years. She managed shipments, organized routes, and trained staff. One morning, her login failed. She emailed IT. They said her role was "no longer active." She called HR. They said, "AI has optimized your department." No one thanked her. No one said goodbye. She didn't quit. She didn't get fired. She simply ceased to exist in the system.

Story with a Lesson

During the COVID-19 pandemic, companies rushed to automate. One retail chain introduced AI inventory systems. Within six months, 200 workers lost jobs. The company issued no mass layoff notice. Instead, it reduced shifts until employees quit out of starvation. The lesson: silent layoffs are more dangerous than loud ones because they leave no evidence, no outrage, no headlines.

Chapter Manifesto

We declare: silent layoffs are violence.

We reject the lie that AI is a "helper." We reject the faceless dismissal of workers. We reject the normalization of human redundancy.

Our manifesto: every system built on labor must answer to labor. A society that replaces humans with code must be confronted, resisted, and rebuilt.

Survival Solutions

Parallel Income

Build ownership outside of jobs before AI erases the job itself.

Community Alerts

Workers must share stories of silent layoffs to expose patterns.

AI Transparency Laws

Push for legislation demanding disclosure of how and when AI displaces workers.

Sovereign Skills

Learn skills that AI cannot replicate easily: leadership, creativity, community-building, manual trades.

Union 2.0

Digital unions that track AI replacements and fight for accountability.

Future Scenario

By 2035, millions of jobs will vanish without a word. Silent layoffs will not come in waves — they will come in drips, invisible and deniable. A whole generation may grow up never hearing the words "you're fired," because they were never hired in the first place.

But resistance will form. Some communities will build AI cooperatives where workers own the tools, not corporations. Others will create local economies immune to automation. The future will not be a war between humans and machines — it will be a war between humans who own the machines and humans who don't.

Prophecy Close & Lesson

The prophecy closes with this: the layoff of the future will not come with drama, anger, or even awareness. It will come in silence. The login won't work. The schedule won't appear. The job will vanish. The silence will be the sound of profit. And unless the people resist, the silence will never end.

Chapter 9: White Collar Is the New Blue Collar

Prophecy Opener

For generations, the office was sold as an escape. The white shirt, the tie, the air-conditioned desk job — these were symbols of safety. Parents told children, "Work with your mind, not your hands, and you'll never struggle." College degrees became the ticket. Cubicles became status. Salaries became shields.

But the prophecy is this: the walls of the office are crumbling, and white-collar jobs are being dragged into the same precarity once reserved for factory floors. Accountants, analysts, paralegals, designers, even doctors — all will discover that automation doesn't care about ties or titles. In the age of AI, the desk becomes a machine, and the worker becomes just another replaceable cog. The myth of white-collar immunity dies here.

Psychological Breakdown

Collapse of Prestige

White-collar work once carried dignity. Losing that prestige erodes personal and social identity. People don't just lose jobs; they lose status.

Student Loan Chains

Millions borrowed heavily for degrees that promised stability. Watching AI outpace their diplomas creates bitterness and despair.

False Security Blanket

For decades, people believed "at least I'm not working with my hands." That belief collapses when the machine outthinks as easily as it outworks.

Fear of Downward Mobility

When office jobs fall, families face falling from suburbs to poverty. Fear of descent chains people tighter than hope of ascent.

Normalization of Overqualification

The PhD becomes the new high school diploma. Lawyers drive Ubers. MBAs work retail. Overqualification stops being rare and starts being normal.

Case Studies & History

Case Study 1: The Legal Industry

AI contract generators already review documents faster than junior lawyers. Entire firms quietly cut entry-level staff, calling it "optimization."

Case Study 2: Accounting Software

Bookkeeping platforms now do in seconds what accountants once billed hours for. Small firms close, larger firms "streamline." The spreadsheet replaces the accountant.

Case Study 3: Marketing and Copywriting

AI tools write ad copy, design campaigns, and even generate logos. Thousands of creative workers are discovering that their "creativity" can be replicated by prompts.

Case Study 4: Telemedicine and Diagnostics

AI medical tools analyze scans with more accuracy than doctors. Human physicians become supervisors of machines instead of trusted decision-makers.

Case Study 5: The Corporate Ladder Collapse

Once, promotions defined careers. Now, flattened structures mean workers stay at the same rung until replaced. The ladder doesn't break — it disappears.

Corporate vs. Street POV

Corporate: "AI frees professionals to focus on higher-value work."
Street: "AI eats the entry-level jobs, and without a bottom rung, no one climbs."

Corporate: "White-collar work will evolve."
Street: "Evolve into what? A gig hustle with a degree price tag."

Corporate: "Education ensures stability."
Street: "Education ensures debt. Stability no longer exists."

Corporate: "Technology creates opportunities."
Street: "Technology creates fewer winners and millions of losers."

Parable

Jonathan graduated with honors in finance. His parents beamed as he stepped into his first office role at a major firm. He bought suits, a car, and believed the ladder was waiting. Five years later, his role was "consolidated into automation." His degree was no shield. He applied for jobs but discovered hundreds of applicants for every opening — many with more experience. Jonathan ended up working in a warehouse while paying $800 a month in student loans. His story wasn't failure — it was prophecy.

Real-Life Story with a Lesson

During the early 2020s, a wave of layoffs hit major tech companies. Engineers and analysts — once considered untouchable elites — flooded LinkedIn with posts about unemployment. Many had six-figure salaries, advanced degrees, and glowing resumes. Yet AI tools had taken over tasks, investors demanded "efficiency," and departments evaporated. The lesson: prestige jobs offer no immunity. White-collar collapse is not a glitch; it's the new model.

Chapter Manifesto

We declare: the office is no sanctuary.

We reject the lie that degrees guarantee stability. We reject the false promise that titles protect against obsolescence. We reject the normalization of overqualification as progress.

Our manifesto: all labor has dignity — but all labor must be sovereign. Office or factory, hand or mind, wage or salary — the only protection is ownership.

Survival Solutions

Diversify Skills Beyond the Desk
Learn trades, arts, leadership, and survival skills. Do not depend solely on degrees.

Leverage AI Instead of Competing
Workers who master AI as a tool — not fear it as a threat — gain leverage.

Build Parallel Incomes
Side hustles, intellectual property, and group economics must supplement collapsing white-collar wages.

Reject Status Worship

Stop chasing prestige and start building sovereignty. A title cannot feed a family.

Community Job Shields

Instead of competing alone, build cooperative structures where displaced workers support each other with pooled resources.

Future Scenario

By 2040, white-collar collapse will be complete. Offices will be smaller, leaner, and more automated. The majority of desk jobs — analysts, clerks, assistants, managers — will not exist. Degrees will no longer guarantee careers, only debt.

But resistance will adapt. Workers will build economies outside of corporate ladders. Communities will reclaim dignity through ownership, not titles. Survival will not be about climbing a disappearing ladder — it will be about building a new foundation.

Prophecy Close & Lesson

The prophecy closes with this: the tie will not save you. The desk will not protect you. The diploma will not guarantee you. White-collar jobs are the new blue-collar grind, and the collapse has already begun. The only security left is not in offices, but in ownership.

Chapter 10: The Disappearing Ladder

Prophecy Opener

The ladder was the promise. Work hard, start at the bottom, climb step by step, and one day you'll reach the top. The American Dream depended on it. The corporate system sold it. Families sacrificed for it. Schools prepared children for it. The ladder was more than promotion — it was hope.

But the prophecy is this: the ladder is disappearing. Promotions are replaced with "expanded responsibilities." Raises shrink into cost-of-living adjustments. Titles inflate without pay. The climb stalls, the rungs vanish, and the workers are left clinging to air. The promise of progress is gone, replaced by plateaus. The dream of upward mobility collapses into a new nightmare: permanent stagnation.

Psychological Breakdown

The Plateau Trap
Workers are told they're "valued" but remain stuck in the same role for years. Stagnation eats at ambition and identity.

Title Inflation Illusion
New titles replace real promotions. "Associate" becomes "specialist," but pay and power don't change. Prestige becomes placebo.

False Sense of Growth
Companies disguise stagnation as "development opportunities," giving more tasks without real compensation.

Exhaustion of Climbing Without Progress

Employees pour energy into a system that refuses to lift them. The grind becomes treadmill: motion without movement.

Psychic Collapse of Aspiration

Without a ladder, ambition becomes despair. People stop dreaming, stop striving, and accept cages as destiny.

Case Studies & History

Case Study 1: The Flat Company Model

Tech firms like to boast "flat structures." In reality, it means no promotions exist. Workers live as permanent "team members," disposable at will.

Case Study 2: The Shrinking Middle Management

In the 1990s, corporations had layers of managers to climb through. Today, automation and "lean teams" cut rungs until workers hit ceilings.

Case Study 3: Wage Stagnation

Since the 1970s, wages barely moved while productivity soared. Workers climbed ladders that led to nowhere.

Case Study 4: Degree Inflation

Jobs that once required a high school diploma now demand bachelor's or master's degrees. The ladder isn't higher — it's fake.

Case Study 5: The Gig Economy Mirage

Gig platforms promise "be your own boss." In reality, there is no ladder — only endless hustling on flat ground.

Corporate vs. Street POV

Corporate: "We offer opportunities for growth."
Street: "You offer more work with no pay."

Corporate: "Our structure is flat to empower collaboration."
Street: "Your flat structure means no one climbs."

Corporate: "Promotions are earned by loyalty."
Street: "Promotions don't exist — just recycled titles."

Corporate: "We're lean and efficient."
Street: "You're cheap and exploitative."

Parable

Luis worked at a bank for twelve years. He trained new hires, carried extra responsibilities, and stayed late without pay. Each year, he was told, "Your dedication is noticed." Each year, the promotion didn't come. Finally, a younger worker was hired with a fancier title, but at the same pay Luis earned. The ladder Luis believed in had never been real. He was climbing rungs painted on the wall.

Real-Life Story with a Lesson

In 2018, employees at a large retail chain discovered that their "promotions" came with no raises. Workers were told titles mattered for "career development." When the company filed bankruptcy, those same "career titles" meant nothing in the job market. The lesson: titles without power are chains disguised as crowns.

Chapter Manifesto

We declare: the ladder is gone.

We reject the lie that stagnation is growth. We reject the illusion of title inflation. We reject the culture that praises motion without movement.

Our manifesto: progress must be real, not symbolic. A ladder that doesn't lead upward is a trap, not a path.

Survival Solutions

Reject Title Illusions

Value real compensation and ownership, not labels that disguise stagnation.

Build Parallel Ladders

Construct growth outside corporations: skills, businesses, and community structures.

Demand Transparency

Force companies to show real promotion and pay metrics. Silence feeds exploitation.

Invest in Yourself, Not Their Ladder

Degrees and loyalty no longer guarantee progress. Put effort into building sovereign assets.

Unite Against Stagnation

Workers must collectively resist unpaid "growth" disguised as opportunity.

Future Scenario

By 2040, ladders will be a myth. Companies will offer "roles" but not "careers." Generations will live in permanent plateaus. Degrees will pile up, wages will stagnate, and millions will realize the ladder was always an illusion.

But resistance will emerge. New ladders will form in communities, cooperatives, and ownership models. Instead of climbing someone else's system, people will build their own.

Prophecy Close & Lesson

The prophecy closes with this: the ladder was never meant to lift you. It was meant to distract you, to keep you climbing without moving. Now the ladder is disappearing, and the illusion collapses. The only climb left is the one you build yourself.

Chapter 11: Labor Without Laborers

Prophecy Opener

The foundation of society was once simple: if something needed to be built, carried, or repaired, human hands did it. The sweat of the worker shaped cities, harvested food, and kept the world alive. Labor was the heartbeat of existence.

But the prophecy is this: the age of AI and robotics will bring labor without laborers. Machines will farm, robots will build, algorithms will manage. The fields will grow without farmers. The warehouses will hum without pickers. The offices will run without clerks. Humanity will watch as the very concept of work is decoupled from human presence. And when labor no longer needs laborers, what becomes of the laborer?

Psychological Breakdown

Loss of Identity

Work has long defined self-worth: "I am a carpenter, I am a teacher, I am a nurse." When machines take those roles, individuals face existential crises.

Collapse of Community Fabric

Shared labor builds bonds — construction crews, farms, classrooms. Automation dissolves those networks, leaving isolation.

Fear of Worthlessness

People fear becoming useless. A society that values only productivity devalues the unneeded human.

Dependency on Systems

As humans lose work, they depend more on machines and the elites who own them. Control deepens.

Alienation

Without labor, people lose rhythm, structure, and purpose. Days blur into despair, feeding addiction and distraction.

Case Studies & History

Case Study 1: The Automated Farm

In California, robots already plant, water, and harvest crops. Migrant labor shrinks, but displaced workers are given no alternatives.

Case Study 2: Self-Driving Trucks

Millions of truck drivers face replacement by autonomous fleets. The trucking industry once fed whole families — soon it may feed only shareholders.

Case Study 3: Construction Robotics

3D-printed houses rise in days, replacing crews of carpenters and masons. Homes appear faster, but workers vanish from payrolls.

Case Study 4: Factories Without Humans

In China and the U.S., "lights-out factories" operate entirely with robots, running 24/7 in darkness because no human is inside.

Case Study 5: Algorithmic Management

Gig platforms prove humans are already half-displaced. Delivery "workers" are managed like machines, and full automation is only a step away.

Corporate vs. Street POV

Corporate: “Automation improves efficiency.”
Street: “Efficiency means erasing us.”

Corporate: “Robots take dangerous jobs.”
Street: “Robots take jobs that kept us alive.”

Corporate: “This is progress.”
Street: “Progress for who? Not for the ones replaced.”

Corporate: “We will retrain displaced workers.”
Street: “Retrain them for what, when machines do it all?”

Parable

Diego’s father was a truck driver for thirty years. He raised four kids hauling freight across highways. Diego followed him, proud to continue the legacy. Then the fleet announced it was going driverless. Diego watched the trucks roll out without cabs. His father said, “They don’t need us anymore.” Diego realized he hadn’t just lost a job — he had lost an identity that stretched across generations.

Real-Life Story with a Lesson

When 3D-printed construction expanded in Mexico and Texas, entire villages were built in weeks with almost no human labor. Crews who once relied on masonry and carpentry were told to “find new trades.” But what new trades exist when machines dominate all? The lesson: automation doesn’t only kill jobs — it kills crafts, cultures, and lineages.

Chapter Manifesto

We declare: labor without laborers is theft of humanity.

We reject the idea that progress means erasing workers. We reject the normalization of machines over men. We reject the erasure of culture, dignity, and purpose.

Our manifesto: labor must honor humans, not erase them. If machines rise, humans must own them. If automation spreads, communities must benefit, not suffer.

Survival Solutions

Ownership of Automation

If machines replace jobs, workers must own shares in the machines. Profit without participation is slavery.

Revaluing Human Skills

Culture must elevate what robots cannot do: creativity, empathy, leadership, resistance.

Parallel Economies

Communities must build local economies where machines do not dominate survival.

Political Pressure

Demand that governments tie automation profits to public benefits. Tax robots, not just humans.

Tribal Reconnection

When work collapses, community must replace lost purpose. Tribe over task.

Future Scenario

By 2050, entire industries may function without human labor. Automated farms, driverless fleets, robotic factories, AI-managed offices. Human work will be optional, not essential. For elites, this will mean endless profit. For workers, it will mean endless despair — unless resistance creates ownership.

The future will not be about stopping automation — it will be about controlling who owns it. Communities that build sovereign AI, cooperative robotics, and shared automation will thrive. Those that remain dependent will collapse.

Prophecy Close & Lesson

The prophecy closes with this: the world is marching toward labor without laborers. The question is not whether machines will replace us. The question is whether we will let elites own the machines alone, or whether we will seize them and make labor serve humanity again.

Chapter 12: Can Everyone Just Learn to Code?

Prophecy Opener

Whenever automation threatens jobs, the elites repeat the same sermon: "Just learn to code." They frame it as a magic solution, a universal escape hatch from the collapse of work. But the prophecy is this: not everyone can code, not everyone should code, and even coding itself will be devoured by automation. The advice is not salvation — it is mockery.

The system tells millions of truck drivers, nurses, janitors, factory workers, and waiters to "learn to code," as if decades of skill, sweat, and sacrifice can be erased and replaced with keyboard strokes. And even those who do master it soon discover that AI writes code faster than they ever could. The lie is exposed: the future cannot be built on one brittle skill.

Psychological Breakdown

The False Hope Narrative
"Coding saves you" becomes a mantra, creating guilt for those who cannot adapt. Workers blame themselves instead of the system.

Cognitive Divide
Not everyone's brain is wired for abstract logic. Forcing millions into coding creates new hierarchies of failure.

Disposable Knowledge
Programming languages shift constantly. Skills are outdated in years, sometimes months. Stability disappears.

The Myth of Meritocracy

"Anyone can learn to code" sounds egalitarian, but it ignores unequal access to time, education, and technology.

Automation Eating Its Own Children

Even skilled coders face replacement. AI writes cleaner, faster, more scalable code. The snake consumes its tail.

Case Studies & History

Case Study 1: The Coding Bootcamp Mirage

In the 2010s, thousands enrolled in coding bootcamps, believing they'd land six-figure jobs. Many graduated into saturated markets, unemployed or underpaid.

Case Study 2: Outsourcing of Software Jobs

U.S. firms outsourced programming overseas. Coders in India or Eastern Europe worked for less, proving coding was no safer than factory labor.

Case Study 3: AI Code Generators

Tools like GitHub Copilot already draft entire functions. Workers discovered the very skill they were told to master was already automated.

Case Study 4: Historical Echo — The Typist Era

In the 20th century, millions learned typing as a profession. Automation erased the career. Coding risks the same fate.

Case Study 5: The College Degree Trap

Computer science degrees ballooned in cost, leaving students in debt. Meanwhile, the demand for entry-level coders collapsed under automation.

Corporate vs. Street POV

Corporate: "Coding is the future of work."
Street: "Coding is already the past — machines do it faster."

Corporate: "Anyone can reinvent themselves with coding."
Street: "That's elitist fantasy. Not everyone has the time, brain, or resources."

Corporate: "The market needs more programmers."
Street: "The market needs fewer humans and more bots."

Corporate: "Bootcamps and degrees will save you."
Street: "Bootcamps and degrees will chain you with debt."

Parable

A trucking company shut down 3,000 jobs when automation arrived. Officials told the drivers, "You can always learn to code." Jamal, a 52-year-old father of four, enrolled in an online bootcamp. He struggled, but finished. By graduation, the job postings required three years of experience and listed salaries slashed by outsourcing. Jamal realized too late: the system didn't want him to win. It wanted him to blame himself for losing.

Real-Life Story with a Lesson

When AI coding assistants launched, many junior developers discovered their workload vanish overnight. Tasks that took weeks now took minutes. Companies cut entry-level staff. Senior programmers leaned on AI to move faster, but the ladder for newcomers disappeared. The lesson: even those who learn to code are not safe. Coding is not the fortress it was promised to be.

Chapter Manifesto

We declare: "Learn to code" is not a solution.

We reject the lie that survival in a collapsing labor market can be solved by forcing millions into one brittle skill. We reject the guilt placed on displaced workers. We reject the erasure of dignity for those who cannot or do not want to code.

Our manifesto: survival must be rooted in sovereignty, not slogans. The future cannot be built on chasing the next hype skill. It must be built on ownership, creativity, and community resilience.

Survival Solutions

Diversify Skills Beyond Coding
Learn trades, storytelling, leadership, agriculture, design — things that AI cannot fully replicate.

Use AI as a Tool, Not an Enemy
Leverage AI coding assistants to enhance, not replace, human problem-solving.

Reject Skill Monopolies
No single skill will save everyone. Communities must value multiple abilities.

Invest in Intellectual Property
Books, art, brands, and culture cannot be replaced by code.

Group Economics

Coding without ownership is just modern labor. Ownership of platforms is survival.

Future Scenario

By 2040, coding as a career will shrink. AI will dominate code-writing, leaving only a fraction of humans in oversight roles. Millions who "learned to code" will discover their efforts wasted. Yet, communities that leverage coding alongside creativity and ownership will thrive. The survivors won't just code — they'll build sovereign systems that AI cannot own.

Prophecy Close & Lesson

The prophecy closes with this: "Learn to code" was never advice — it was mockery. It was the system's way of saying, "You are replaceable." Coding will not save the masses. Only sovereignty will.

Chapter 13: The Rise of the AI Lords

Prophecy Opener

The new kings will not wear crowns — they will own servers. They will not sit on thrones — they will sit behind code. The AI Lords will not rule with swords, but with algorithms that dictate life, labor, and law. The prophecy is this: in the age of artificial intelligence, power will consolidate into the hands of a few corporations and billionaires who own the data, the machines, and the infrastructure.

We are entering a feudal system reborn. In the past, lords owned land and peasants worked it. In the future, AI Lords will own data and the rest of us will feed it. And just like serfs, we may find ourselves bound to digital estates — unable to escape, always producing, never truly free.

Psychological Breakdown

Dependency Creation
AI tools become "essential." Once hooked, people cannot imagine working, shopping, or thinking without them.

Invisible Rule
Unlike kings of old, AI Lords don't need armies. Their rule is silent — through pricing models, algorithms, and terms of service.

The Illusion of Choice
Users believe they are free because apps are optional. But every option routes back to a handful of AI-powered monopolies.

The Data Feudalism Trap

People give up privacy in exchange for convenience. This is the new tithe — not crops, but clicks.

Fear Conditioning

Workers fear obsolescence, companies fear irrelevance, nations fear being left behind. The AI Lords thrive on that fear.

Case Studies & History

Case Study 1: Big Tech Monopolies

Google, Amazon, Microsoft, and Apple dominate cloud infrastructure. AI models depend on their compute power. Independent developers become vassals.

Case Study 2: Subscription Serfdom

AI tools are packaged as monthly subscriptions. The population becomes addicted. A single company shutting down an API can cripple thousands of livelihoods.

Case Study 3: Data Colonization

Social media firms trained AI on billions of users' photos, posts, and art without consent. The peasants tilled the land; the lords claimed the harvest.

Case Study 4: Historical Echo — Feudal Lords of Europe

Medieval peasants worked land they did not own. Modern workers generate data they do not own. The structure is the same; only the harvest changed.

Case Study 5: National Sovereignty vs. AI Lords

Governments rely on corporate AI to run surveillance, defense, and administration. Nations become clients, not rulers.

Corporate vs. Street POV

Corporate: “AI empowers everyone.”
Street: “AI empowers whoever owns it.”

Corporate: “The future is open.”
Street: “The future is fenced off like private land.”

Corporate: “These tools level the playing field.”
Street: “These tools raise the floor for the few and trap the rest underneath it.”

Corporate: “AI is neutral.”
Street: “No master’s tool is ever neutral.”

Parable

In a small town, a farmer once fed his family from his own land. When the land was seized by a landlord, he had to pay rent with most of his harvest. Centuries later, Malik uploads his songs to a platform. The platform uses his music to train AI, which then generates endless songs without him. Malik is forced to pay the platform to promote his own work. The land changed; the chains did not.

Real-Life Story with a Lesson

Artists in 2023 discovered AI art trained on their work. Their brushstrokes, styles, and signatures were replicated by machines that erased their names. Lawsuits rose, but the lesson was clear: ownership of the algorithm mattered more than talent. The AI Lords did not need to steal paintings; they only needed to steal patterns.

Chapter Manifesto

We declare: AI without sovereignty is slavery.

We reject the feudal future where power is concentrated in data lords. We reject the theft of human creativity for corporate profit. We reject the illusion of access while ownership is denied.

Our manifesto: the people must own their data, their platforms, and their future. AI cannot be allowed to become another empire where the majority labor for the wealth of the few.

Survival Solutions

Build Cooperative AI Models
Communities must pool resources to create and own their own AI tools.

Demand Data Rights
Fight for laws that make individuals owners of their data, not products of it.

Group Economics Against AI Lords
If individuals cannot fight monopolies, communities can. Collective ownership is the only shield.

Hybrid Sovereignty
Use AI tools strategically, but never depend on one company. Spread risk across platforms.

Cultural Resistance
Preserve human creativity and community as sacred spaces machines cannot colonize.

Future Scenario

By 2050, the AI Lords may control energy grids, food systems, education, healthcare, and governance. Nations may shrink into provinces of corporate AI empires. Yet, there will also be pockets of rebellion: self-sufficient communities running open-source AI on local servers, guarded like sacred wells.

History teaches us this: empires fall when people refuse their chains. If AI Lords rise unchecked, the future will belong to them. But if people reclaim ownership, the Lords will become servants — and the balance will shift.

Prophecy Close & Lesson

The prophecy closes with this: AI Lords are not coming — they are already here. The question is not whether they will rise, but whether we will kneel.

Chapter 14: When Work No Longer Buys Survival

Prophecy Opener

There was a time when a paycheck could keep a roof overhead, food on the table, and dignity in the home. That time is gone. The prophecy is this: the day is coming when a lifetime of labor will not guarantee survival. Wages will shrink, costs will rise, and the math will break until even the hardest workers cannot hold the line.

In this age, working forty hours won't mean food security. Two jobs won't mean stability. Three jobs won't mean freedom. Work will become a ritual — performed, repeated, exhausted — but no longer rewarded. The machine will demand endless output and give nothing in return. The old contract — labor in exchange for life — will collapse.

Psychological Breakdown

The Broken Exchange
People are conditioned to believe labor = survival. When wages stagnate and inflation rises, the equation breaks, but the conditioning keeps them grinding.

The Guilt Trap
Workers blame themselves when survival slips, not the system. They are told they didn't hustle hard enough, didn't learn the right skill, didn't adapt fast enough.

The Fear of Irrelevance
AI and automation erode the value of labor. A man's trade is replaced by a machine, a woman's desk job by software. Identity collapses with income.

Psychological Inflation

Prices rising faster than wages make survival feel like drowning. Each raise is swallowed, each bonus already spent. People live on the edge of panic.

The New Poverty of Time

When survival costs more, workers sell more hours. Even rest becomes unaffordable. People die younger because survival demands their life span as payment.

Case Studies & History

Case Study 1: Weimar Germany (1920s)

Hyperinflation made wages meaningless. Workers were paid twice a day, rushing to spend money before it lost value. Survival detached from work.

Case Study 2: The American Worker (1970s–Today)

Since the 1970s, productivity tripled while wages stagnated. Work produced more wealth, but none of it returned to workers.

Case Study 3: The Gig Worker in 2020s America

Delivery drivers earning less than minimum wage after expenses. Nurses working double shifts with no benefits. "Independent contractor" became code for disposable labor.

Case Study 4: Historical Echo — The Great Depression

Men lined up for bread after farms collapsed and banks failed. They had skills, they had labor, but labor couldn't buy survival.

Case Study 5: Modern Rent Crisis

Rent rises faster than income in every major city. Families with two jobs still live in shelters. Work has lost its purchasing power.

Corporate vs. Street POV

Corporate: “Workers need to upskill.”
Street: “You can’t upskill your way out of robbery.”

Corporate: “Hard work pays off.”
Street: “Hard work pays them, not you.”

Corporate: “Inflation is temporary.”
Street: “Poverty is permanent when wages stay frozen.”

Corporate: “The market decides value.”
Street: “The market decides who gets robbed first.”

Parable

Jorge worked sixty hours a week in two kitchens. His hands were scarred from grease burns, his back bent from lifting crates. He dreamed of saving for a house. But rent rose, groceries doubled, gas tripled. Each month, the landlord took more, the store charged more, the debt collectors called more. One night, Jorge calculated: he had worked 280 hours that month. After bills, he had $12 left. His labor bought survival for others, but not for him.

Real-Life Story with a Lesson

In 2023, Amazon warehouse workers reported skipping meals to cover rising rent. They worked for one of the richest companies in the world, yet lived in cars or tents outside the facility. The lesson: working for wealth does not mean access to wealth. In the machine's logic, survival is not guaranteed by labor — it is rented back at a premium.

Chapter Manifesto

We declare: labor that cannot buy survival is slavery by another name.

We reject the myth that wages are fair. We reject the lie that more hustle means more security. We reject the system where survival costs outpace human effort.

Our manifesto: survival is a right, not a privilege. Work should sustain life, not consume it. If the system cannot honor this, the system must fall.

Survival Solutions

Community Economies

Shared housing, co-ops, and community gardens reduce survival costs. Pooling resources fights inflation.

Ownership First

Shift from working for wages to building streams of ownership: side hustles, digital assets, land, and group investments.

Skill Sovereignty

Learn skills that serve community survival: farming, mechanics, tailoring, coding. Skills that cannot be automated are shields.

Collective Bargaining

Workers uniting for living wages, not minimum wages, change the survival equation.

Exit the Rat Race

Build side exits from the wage economy. Even partial independence from survival costs builds leverage.

Future Scenario

By 2040, wages may lose 70% of their value against living costs. A job will no longer buy shelter, food, or healthcare. Survival will require multiple incomes, collective ownership, or total dependency on corporate housing and ration systems.

The risk: people reduced to digital serfs — working just to earn corporate credits redeemable only in their employer's ecosystem. The promise: if communities build sovereign survival networks now, the collapse will not crush them.

Prophecy Close & Lesson

The prophecy closes with this: when work no longer buys survival, survival must be built outside of work. Labor is no longer the path to life — ownership, community, and sovereignty are.

Chapter 15: The Housing Mirage — Real Estate When Wages Collapse

Prophecy Opener

They told you buying a home was the cornerstone of freedom. They told you renting was a step on the ladder to ownership. They told you housing was security. But the prophecy is this: in the age of collapsing wages, housing becomes the new shackle. Mortgages become chains heavier than iron, rent becomes a lifelong tax, and ownership turns into a mirage that disappears the closer you walk toward it.

The system has no interest in you owning land — it wants you paying forever. The landlord class thrives on your dependency. The banks thrive on your signatures. The government thrives on inflated taxes. And when AI eats jobs, when wages can no longer keep up, housing will not protect you — it will imprison you.

Psychological Breakdown

The Dream Deferred
Workers are programmed to believe homeownership equals arrival. When wages collapse, they keep chasing the dream even when the numbers don't work.

Rent Serfdom
Rent is designed to rise faster than wages. This forces workers to run in place — labor is consumed just to keep a roof overhead.

Debt Worship
Mortgages are sold as investment but function as decades-long servitude. People are taught to celebrate debt as if it were wealth.

Fear of Homelessness

Housing insecurity keeps workers compliant. No one risks speaking out at work if it means missing rent.

Illusion of Equity

Even when homes rise in value, taxes, insurance, and maintenance eat the profit. Equity exists on paper but not in pockets.

Case Studies & History

Case Study 1: The Subprime Crisis (2008)

Banks handed out loans to people they knew couldn't pay. When wages and jobs collapsed, millions lost homes. The dream turned into eviction notices.

Case Study 2: Rent in the 2020s

In Los Angeles, median rent reached $2,900/month while median wages stayed below $60k/year. Housing ate over half of income. Survival was consumed by landlords.

Case Study 3: Historical Tenant Farming

Sharecroppers worked land they never owned. Generations labored without wealth accumulation. Modern renters live the same cycle — labor in, nothing kept.

Case Study 4: Corporate Landlords

BlackRock and other giants buy entire neighborhoods, renting homes back to families who can no longer compete. Ownership shifts from people to corporations.

Case Study 5: Future Ghost Homes

In cities like Vancouver and Miami, investment properties sit empty while families sleep in cars. Homes become safety deposit boxes for the rich, not shelter for the working.

Corporate vs. Street POV

Corporate: “Housing is a stable investment.”
Street: “Housing is a hustle — you pay, they profit.”

Corporate: “Homeownership is the American Dream.”
Street: “The dream is rigged — the bank owns the deed until you’re dead.”

Corporate: “Rent increases are just the market.”
Street: “The market is the landlord robbing you every 30 days.”

Corporate: “Equity builds wealth.”
Street: “Equity is a carrot — you don’t eat paper wealth when bills are due.”

Parable

Tasha worked two jobs to finally qualify for a mortgage. The bank approved her, but the payments ate 60% of her income. For ten years she paid faithfully. Then a layoff came. Within months, the bank repossessed the home. Tasha looked back and realized: she never owned it. She rented from the bank with the illusion of ownership. The title was hers only until she stumbled.

Real-Life Story with a Lesson

In 2022, a Detroit family paid rent for 18 years in the same home. They assumed they’d “earned it.” When the landlord died, his heirs sold the property to an out-of-state investor. The family was evicted in 60 days. The lesson: without ownership, decades of rent vanish into nothing. Labor buys survival but never security.

Chapter Manifesto

We declare: housing is not freedom when it is debt.

We reject the lie that mortgages equal wealth. We reject the theft that is rising rent without rising wages. We reject the illusion that the American Dream was ever about ownership for the working class.

Our manifesto: land belongs to the people who live on it. Shelter is a human right, not a landlord's lottery ticket. True survival requires collective control of land and homes, not endless dependency.

Survival Solutions

Community Land Trusts

Groups purchase land and hold it in trust for permanent affordability. No corporate landlord can evict what the community owns.

Cooperative Housing

Residents own shares of the property together. No single family carries the full burden, and profit doesn't bleed out to banks.

Debt Resistance

Organized refusal to pay exploitative rents and mortgages forces renegotiation and relief.

Micro-Ownership

Families pooling resources to buy duplexes, trailers, or small parcels to build sovereignty.

Rent-to-Own Collectives

Turning rent payments into equity by demanding contracts that build ownership instead of burning wages.

Future Scenario

By 2050, homeownership rates may drop below 40%. Entire generations will never own property. Land will consolidate under corporate landlords who rent survival back at inflated rates. Cities will become fortresses of investment homes while workers sprawl in collapsing suburbs or car encampments.

But resistance rises: sovereign communities purchase acreage together, living debt-free in mobile structures, farming their land, and rejecting mortgages. Housing becomes less about McMansions and more about survival-first compounds. The future belongs to those who build shelter outside the system's reach.

Prophecy Close & Lesson

The prophecy closes with this: housing as we know it is not freedom — it is feudalism with paperwork. To survive, you must strip the illusion from the dream. Don't chase what was never meant for you. Build what they cannot take: land shared, land protected, land lived on as community. Only then does housing stop being a mirage.

Chapter 16: The Ghost Town Economy — Malls, Offices, Schools Left Behind

Prophecy Opener

They promised you growth. They promised every town would have its mall, its main street, its office park, its school district that guaranteed stability. But the prophecy is this: when wages collapse and AI hollows out the labor market, the landscape of America itself collapses.

The malls turn into mausoleums. Offices become relics. Schools stand half-empty, teaching curriculums built for jobs that no longer exist. Ghost towns don't just live in deserts — they rise in suburbs, in cities, in once-booming communities.

The prophecy is clear: capitalism doesn't care about communities, only transactions. When the money leaves, the system leaves too — and people are abandoned among the shells of an economy that no longer exists.

Psychological Breakdown

The Promise of Permanence
People were conditioned to believe their local institutions — schools, malls, offices — were permanent. Seeing them vanish causes disorientation and despair.

The Loss of Place
When physical centers close, people lose a sense of belonging. The community fractures into individuals, easier to control.

Economic Amnesia

Workers are told closures are temporary or cyclical. But collapse repeats and deepens, making denial easier than resistance.

Fear of Irrelevance

As institutions crumble, workers fear they too are obsolete. The closing of buildings mirrors the closing of opportunity.

The Illusion of Progress

Even as closures spread, digital companies present collapse as "innovation." Malls dying? That's "the online marketplace." Schools shrinking? That's "personalized learning." Progress becomes a mask for decay.

Case Studies & History

Case Study 1: The Fall of Sears and the Mall Economy

Once the backbone of middle-class consumption, Sears and other anchors collapsed, dragging entire malls into vacancy. Towns that relied on mall traffic saw restaurants, salons, and local shops wither.

Case Study 2: Rust Belt Factories

Factories that built cars and steel now sit as rusted skeletons. Whole towns — Flint, Gary, Youngstown — became testaments to what happens when capital abandons labor.

Case Study 3: The Pandemic Work-from-Home Shift

COVID accelerated office collapse. Downtown skyscrapers emptied, workers never returned, small businesses that fed off office workers died.

Case Study 4: School Enrollment Decline

With birth rates dropping and education disconnected from survival, schools face closures. Empty classrooms become warehouses, or simply rot.

Case Study 5: Future AI Displacement

As AI replaces both blue- and white-collar jobs, physical spaces tied to labor — call centers, retail stores, offices — collapse in waves. Cities become haunted by their own infrastructure.

Corporate vs. Street POV

Corporate: “Retail is evolving online.”

Street: “You shut down the town and left us with nothing but Wi-Fi bills.”

Corporate: “Remote work is innovation.”

Street: “Remote work killed downtown and the businesses that fed off it.”

Corporate: “Education is going digital.”

Street: “Kids stare at screens while schools decay into prisons.”

Corporate: “Vacant buildings are redevelopment opportunities.”

Street: “They’re monuments to greed — proof you used us and left.”

Parable

Derrick’s hometown mall was once where everyone gathered. He bought sneakers there, ate fries with friends, kissed his first girlfriend in the parking lot. Twenty years later, it’s empty. The roof leaks, weeds push through asphalt, only a dollar store survives. Derrick walks through and realizes: the mall didn't just die — the heartbeat of his town died. Without jobs, without gathering places, the community became strangers sharing empty space.

Real-Life Story with a Lesson

In Ohio, a teacher watched her school shrink year after year. First, the library closed. Then, sports teams disappeared. Then, the district shut down the high school altogether. Kids were bussed an hour away. The teacher said: "We didn't just lose a school. We lost our glue." The lesson: when institutions collapse, community bonds collapse too.

Chapter Manifesto

We declare: empty buildings are not progress.

We reject the lie that malls dying means efficiency. We reject the digital utopia narrative that ignores abandoned communities. We reject the idea that the collapse of schools and offices is natural evolution.

Our manifesto: community is not disposable. We fight for land, for institutions, for spaces that belong to us, not to corporations that leave when the profit dries up.

Survival Solutions

Community Reclamation Projects

Turn abandoned malls into co-ops, housing, or community centers. Don't let decay stay in corporate hands.

Micro-Economies

Build businesses that can thrive without massive infrastructure — local farms, barter networks, shared maker spaces.

Education Reinvention

Transform closed schools into centers for trade learning, survival skills, and independent study for real-world resilience.

Occupy the Empty

Use abandoned office buildings for housing the homeless, studios, and community defense hubs.

Decentralized Gathering

When formal spaces collapse, rebuild informal ones — barbershops, backyards, small churches — as nodes of resilience.

Future Scenario

By 2040, America will be filled with hollow shells: malls repurposed as Amazon warehouses, schools converted into condos, offices demolished for luxury apartments no one can afford. The ghost town economy spreads, leaving islands of hyper-wealth surrounded by oceans of abandonment.

But resistance grows: communities purchase dead malls at pennies, turning them into sovereign compounds — with housing, gardens, gyms, and trade schools. Ghost towns become reclaimed towns. The lesson: collapse can destroy or create, depending on who seizes the ruins.

Prophecy Close & Lesson

The prophecy closes with this: the ghost town is not an accident. It is the blueprint of a system that extracts, abandons, and repeats. You cannot beg a system to revive what it has already buried. You must take the ruins and rebuild your own economy. Only then do ghost towns become living towns again.

Chapter 17: Healthcare Without Humans — AI Doctors vs. Those Without Coverage

Prophecy Opener

They told you the doctor would save you. They told you hospitals were temples of healing. They told you the system cared about health. But the prophecy is this: in the age of AI, healthcare splits into two realities.

One reality: AI-powered clinics that can scan, diagnose, and prescribe faster than any human doctor. The wealthy plug in, monitor in real-time, and live longer than history ever allowed.

The other reality: the poor locked out of access, left to rot in overworked hospitals, or denied altogether. Healthcare without humans doesn't mean universal healing — it means automation of exclusion. Technology becomes the new scalpel that divides the classes.

Psychological Breakdown

False Security

People cling to the belief that medical advances mean everyone benefits. In truth, advances widen inequality.

Dependency Programming

Workers are conditioned to trust "the system" with their health. That dependency makes collapse devastating when access is cut off.

Fear of the Bill

For the poor, sickness isn't just about survival — it's about debt. Fear of bankruptcy keeps people from seeking care until it's too late.

Illusion of Progress

AI promises efficiency but hides the real tradeoff: profit over healing. Efficiency serves corporations, not patients.

Dehumanization of Healing

Patients become data points. Care becomes metrics. Humanity is stripped from medicine in the name of speed.

Case Studies & History

Case Study 1: The Affordable Care Mirage

Obamacare expanded access, but deductibles and premiums still crushed working families. The illusion of universal care masked a reality of limited survival.

Case Study 2: The Pandemic Divide

COVID showed two systems: the wealthy with private doctors and testing, the poor lined up outside overwhelmed hospitals. Survival depended on money, not medicine.

Case Study 3: AI in Radiology

Algorithms now outperform human radiologists in identifying tumors. But access is limited to elite hospitals, leaving rural and poor communities decades behind.

Case Study 4: Insulin in America

A life-saving drug costs $5 to produce, but $300+ to buy. AI can optimize distribution, but corporations keep the chokehold. Profit trumps survival.

Case Study 5: Historical Precedent — Tuskegee

Black men were denied treatment for syphilis in the name of "study." History proves the system will experiment on the poor while protecting the wealthy. AI will only scale this divide.

Corporate vs. Street POV

Corporate: “AI will democratize healthcare.”
Street: “AI will privatize healthcare — the rich get robots, the poor get waiting rooms.”

Corporate: “Data-driven medicine increases accuracy.”
Street: “They turn you into data, sell your body back to you, and call it care.”

Corporate: “Healthcare is advancing faster than ever.”
Street: “Advancing for who? The man with money, or the mother with Medicaid?”

Corporate: “Robots will fill the doctor shortage.”
Street: “Robots will replace care for profit, not for compassion.”

Parable

Jamal went to the ER with chest pain. The AI system scanned him in minutes and flagged a possible heart issue. But because he lacked insurance, the hospital discharged him with a $2,000 bill and no treatment. Three weeks later, Jamal died at home. The machine saw him. The system ignored him. Technology cannot replace compassion when the gatekeeper is money.

Real-Life Story with a Lesson

Maria, a single mother in Texas, rationed insulin because her job didn't offer health insurance. AI apps existed that could monitor and adjust her dosage automatically, but they were only available to patients with premium plans. She died at 34 from a preventable complication. The lesson: technology doesn't erase inequality — it magnifies it.

Chapter Manifesto

We declare: healthcare without humans cannot mean healthcare without heart.

We reject the lie that technology will save everyone equally. We reject the false promise that AI alone will heal the broken system. We reject a future where machines care for data but not for people.

Our manifesto: healing must be collective, compassionate, and community-based. Survival means reclaiming medicine from corporations and building systems where access is not sold.

Survival Solutions

Community Clinics

Build grassroots health centers with volunteer professionals and low-cost AI tools. Decentralize medicine from corporate hospitals.

Medical Co-ops

Families and communities pool money for shared health funds to pay for treatment outside the insurance racket.

DIY Health Monitoring

Low-cost devices and open-source AI tools must be hacked and repurposed for community use, not elite hospitals.

Health Education

Teach preventative care, natural remedies, and body awareness. The less dependent you are on a rigged system, the longer you survive.

Pressure Campaigns

Organized movements demanding open access to AI health tech, breaking patents and fighting monopolies.

Future Scenario

By 2050, the wealthy will have AI "guardian angels" — implants, apps, and devices tracking every heartbeat and predicting every disease. The poor will still be waiting in overcrowded clinics, where broken machines replace absent doctors.

But some communities resist. They hack AI tools, share them freely, and train their own local "health hackers" to keep people alive. Health sovereignty becomes survival: the ability to monitor, heal, and prevent without waiting for permission from a system that profits from sickness.

Prophecy Close & Lesson

The prophecy closes with this: healthcare without humans is not salvation — it is segregation. If we don't seize control of the tools, medicine becomes just another wall between the rich and poor. The lesson: don't wait for the system to heal you. Build your own medicine, your own clinics, your own survival networks. Healing belongs to the people, not the machine.

Chapter 18: The Broken Promise of Education — College Debt vs. AI Job Wipeouts

Prophecy Opener

They told you school was the key. They told you college was the ticket. They told you education was the one investment that could never betray you. But the prophecy is this: in the age of AI, education betrays millions.

Degrees become shackles of debt. Diplomas become receipts of obedience. Students emerge into a labor market already claimed by machines, fighting for jobs that no longer exist. The promise of education collapses into a trap: four years in classrooms, forty years in debt, and still no seat at the table.

The prophecy is clear: education was not designed to free the masses — it was designed to sort, filter, and produce obedient labor. Now, with AI replacing labor itself, the machine of schooling grinds on, selling dreams it cannot deliver.

Psychological Breakdown

The Myth of Meritocracy
Students are told if they work hard, they'll rise. But the system rewards wealth, not effort. The poor buy hope with loans; the rich buy access with cash.

Debt as Discipline
Student loans keep graduates locked into jobs they hate. Debt ensures compliance, punishing risk-taking and entrepreneurship.

Credential Worship

Society conditions people to treat diplomas like sacred documents. When jobs vanish, the credential still chains them with interest rates and shame.

Fear of Failure

Dropping out is painted as doom. Students cling to school even when the costs outweigh the benefits. Fear blinds them to alternatives.

Illusion of Preparation

Schools prepare students for a past economy — office jobs, factory roles, steady careers. AI wipes those out, leaving graduates with irrelevant training.

Case Studies & History

Case Study 1: The Student Loan Crisis

$1.7 trillion in U.S. student debt shackles over 45 million people. Degrees promised freedom; debt delivered chains.

Case Study 2: The For-Profit College Scam

Universities like Corinthian sold dreams to poor students, then collapsed, leaving graduates with worthless degrees and massive loans.

Case Study 3: AI Job Elimination

Fields once considered safe — law, accounting, medicine — now face AI disruption. A $150,000 law degree may not protect against an algorithm that drafts contracts for pennies.

Case Study 4: Generational Divide

Boomers could pay for college with a summer job. Millennials and Gen Z face decades of repayment, often for jobs that don't exist.

Case Study 5: Historical Apprenticeships

Before the industrial school model, knowledge came through apprenticeship — learning directly from practice. Debt-free, skill-based, and connected to survival. The past shows a way forward.

Corporate vs. Street POV

Corporate: “Education is an investment in your future.”

Street: “The investment pays the bank, not the graduate.”

Corporate: “College teaches critical thinking.”

Street: “College teaches compliance — sit, listen, obey, pay.”

Corporate: “Degrees increase lifetime earnings.”

Street: “Earnings collapse when robots take the jobs the degree was for.”

Corporate: “Debt is manageable with a good career.”

Street: “The career died before the ink dried.”

Parable

Kevin graduated with a degree in journalism. He owed $90,000 in loans. By the time he finished, AI systems wrote news stories faster and cheaper than humans. Newspapers folded, jobs evaporated. Kevin now drives for delivery apps, still owing $800 a month. His diploma hangs on the wall like a trophy from a war he lost.

Real-Life Story with a Lesson

A Black family in Atlanta put everything into sending their daughter to nursing school. She graduated top of her class. By the time she entered the workforce, hospitals had begun outsourcing diagnostics to AI systems, cutting staff to the bone. She worked longer hours with less pay, her degree worth less each year. The family realized the system wasn't broken — it worked exactly as designed: to extract, not to empower.

Chapter Manifesto

We declare: education is not freedom when it is debt.

We reject the lie that schooling prepares us for survival. We reject the illusion that diplomas guarantee stability. We reject the exploitation of young people's dreams as a profit center for banks and universities.

Our manifesto: education must be redefined as skill, wisdom, and survival — not tuition, debt, and obedience.

Survival Solutions

Trade Sovereignty

Learn trades and survival skills outside institutional systems: carpentry, coding, farming, mechanics. Skills cannot be foreclosed.

Debt Resistance

Organized refusal to repay predatory loans forces system reform. Collectives can fight banks better than individuals.

Community Academies

Communities create their own teaching centers — financial literacy, trade schools, spiritual knowledge. Learning without corporate tuition.

Skill Stacking

Combine multiple skills (digital + physical) to build resilience. An AI can't replace a hustler who codes, farms, and sells.

Parental Resistance

Stop pushing children into debt-based universities. Guide them toward survival education instead of wage slavery.

Future Scenario

By 2050, elite schools will use AI to provide personalized, luxury education to the wealthy — tailored curriculums, private tutors, global networks. For everyone else, "education" will be cheap online programs designed to produce gig workers.

But a third path emerges: underground academies, trade collectives, and sovereign schools where people teach survival, culture, and independence. Communities reclaim education not as a pipeline to jobs — but as training for liberation.

Prophecy Close & Lesson

The prophecy closes with this: the broken promise of education is not an accident — it is the foundation. The system was never meant to free you. It was meant to funnel you into debt and dependency. The lesson is clear: do not confuse schooling with wisdom. Education that does not prepare you for survival is indoctrination. Only by breaking free from the promise and building our own schools can we prepare for the world AI has already created.

Chapter 19: The Vanishing Middle Class — Psychological Breakdown: Denial, Anger, Collapse

Prophecy Opener

They told you the middle class was the backbone of America. They told you if you worked hard, paid taxes, and played by the rules, you'd always belong. They told you the system would protect you. But the prophecy is this: the middle class was never permanent — it was a stage set. A temporary illusion designed to keep workers loyal.

Now, as AI devours jobs, wages stagnate, and debt grows, the middle class vanishes. Families who thought themselves safe are slipping downward, one paycheck, one medical bill, one foreclosure at a time. Denial turns to anger, anger turns to collapse. The prophecy is clear: the middle class was not built to last. It was built to distract, to keep people from rebelling until the system no longer needed them.

Psychological Breakdown

Denial of Decline

Middle-class families cling to the belief they're safe. They keep up appearances — cars, vacations, homes — even as debt swallows them.

Fear of Falling

The middle class lives in terror of becoming poor. That fear drives them to overwork, overspend, and overcomply with systems that are collapsing.

Anger at the Wrong Targets

Instead of aiming at corporations and banks, anger is redirected toward immigrants, minorities, or the poor — divide and conquer psychology.

Collapse of Identity

The middle class ties identity to stability: a home, a career, retirement savings. When these vanish, so does the sense of self.

Comfort Addiction

Even in crisis, middle-class families cling to comfort spending: streaming services, fast food, brand loyalty. Addiction blinds them from the urgency of collapse.

Case Studies & History

Case Study 1: The Housing Bubble (2008)

Millions of middle-class families thought their homes were investments. When the bubble burst, equity vanished overnight. Comfort turned into foreclosure.

Case Study 2: Wage Stagnation vs. Inflation

Since the 1970s, wages barely moved, but costs of housing, healthcare, and education skyrocketed. The illusion of growth masked financial quicksand.

Case Study 3: The Shrinking Middle

In 1971, 61% of Americans were middle class. By 2021, only 50% remained. The middle class literally shrank into history.

Case Study 4: AI Job Threats

Office jobs once reserved for the middle class — accounting, journalism, HR — are now vulnerable to AI automation. Salaries disappear, replaced by gig scraps.

Case Study 5: Historical Precedent — Rome's Collapse

Rome's middle class of tradesmen and farmers vanished under taxes, corruption, and automation by slave labor. The pattern repeats with machines.

Corporate vs. Street POV

Corporate: "The middle class is resilient."
Street: "The middle class is shrinking faster than your paycheck."

Corporate: "Education secures your place."
Street: "Education chains you in debt while jobs vanish."

Corporate: "Homeownership builds security."
Street: "The bank owns your home until you miss a payment."

Corporate: "The system is working."
Street: "It's working for them, not you."

Parable

Lisa and Marcus both had middle-class jobs — she was a teacher, he was a postal worker. Together they made $90,000 a year. They bought a home, leased two cars, and took vacations. But when Marcus was laid off, the numbers crumbled. Bills mounted, credit cards maxed out, foreclosure notices came. Lisa realized: they hadn't been middle class at all. They'd been renting an identity with borrowed money.

Real-Life Story with a Lesson

A factory worker in Ohio saved for years to put his daughter through college. She graduated with $70,000 in debt but no job in her field. The father lost his pension when the factory downsized. Both generations thought they were middle class. Both collapsed into working-poor reality. The lesson: the middle class was never wealth — it was borrowed time.

Chapter Manifesto

We declare: the middle class is not a class — it is a mirage.

We reject the illusion that homeownership, college, and careers guarantee safety. We reject the lie that obedience to the system preserves stability. We reject the fantasy that comfort spending equals wealth.

Our manifesto: survival requires breaking the illusion, abandoning middle-class identity, and preparing for collapse with ownership, skills, and collective power.

Survival Solutions

Downshift with Intent

Don't wait to be forced downward — scale down expenses and debt now to reclaim control.

Collective Housing Models

Share ownership, utilities, and costs with trusted community. Reduces vulnerability when wages shrink.

Asset Reallocation

Sell depreciating consumer goods (cars, gadgets) and reinvest in assets that provide survival (land, tools, trade skills).

Community Wealth Pools

Middle-class families can preserve wealth by pooling resources: childcare, food, repairs. Shared burden, shared strength.

Identity Rebuild

Detach identity from “middle-class” labels. Build identity around sovereignty, resilience, and skill.

Future Scenario

By 2040, the “middle class” may exist only in history books. Cities will split into two castes: the ultra-rich in gated compounds and the working poor surviving paycheck to paycheck. Suburbs become ghost belts of foreclosed homes.

But resistance grows. Former middle-class families band together, creating enclaves of shared housing, pooled savings, and community schools. The label “middle class” disappears — but new tribes of survival replace it, rejecting illusions and building sovereignty.

Prophecy Close & Lesson

The prophecy closes with this: the middle class was never built to save you. It was built to pacify you. The lesson is this: don’t cling to a collapsing identity. Build a new one. Prepare for the fall by embracing survival over illusion. Only then can collapse turn into rebirth.

Chapter 20: Addicted to Distraction — The Man Scrolling While His House Burns

Prophecy Opener

They told you technology would connect you. They told you entertainment was harmless. They told you distraction was just leisure. But the prophecy is this: distraction has become the drug that keeps you docile while the system burns your house down around you.

Screens glow while wages collapse. Notifications buzz while freedoms vanish. People scroll endlessly, fed dopamine while their future dissolves. The prophecy is clear: distraction is not entertainment — it is anesthesia. The man scrolling while his house burns is not fiction. It is our reality.

Psychological Breakdown

The Dopamine Trap
Social media platforms are engineered like slot machines — unpredictable rewards keep people hooked, unable to stop even as life collapses around them.

Attention Colonization
Your focus is the new oil. Every click, swipe, and scroll is extracted, sold, and monetized while you believe you are "choosing."

Escapism Addiction
The harder survival becomes, the more people escape into distraction. Debt, wage loss, and inequality drive deeper screen dependency.

Illusion of Control

Distraction convinces people they're informed because they consume content, when in reality they're numbed and manipulated.

Fear of Silence

Most cannot sit with reality. Noise and distraction replace reflection. Without silence, rebellion cannot form.

Case Studies & History

Case Study 1: The Bread and Circus of Rome

Rome pacified its collapsing empire by distracting the masses with games and feasts. Today's gladiators are influencers, athletes, and Netflix series.

Case Study 2: The Smartphone Era

On average, Americans check their phones 96 times per day. Distraction is no longer leisure — it is the backbone of capitalism.

Case Study 3: The Attention Economy

Facebook, TikTok, and YouTube profit not from content but from capturing human time and selling it to advertisers. Distraction has become currency.

Case Study 4: Political Collapse and Screens

During financial crises, citizens were more engaged with viral trends than with legislation that stole their pensions. Governments thrive on a distracted population.

Case Study 5: Pandemic Escapism

During COVID lockdowns, Netflix and gaming profits exploded. Distraction industries thrived while millions lost jobs and savings.

Corporate vs. Street POV

Corporate: “Entertainment keeps people happy.”
Street: “Entertainment keeps people asleep while their pockets are picked.”

Corporate: “Distraction is choice.”
Street: “Distraction is engineered — every click is designed to keep you weak.”

Corporate: “Screens connect the world.”
Street: “Screens isolate us while corporations collect our data.”

Corporate: “Distraction is harmless fun.”
Street: “Distraction is the leash you don’t even see.”

Parable

Marcus sat scrolling TikTok late into the night, laughing at memes. Outside, his landlord taped an eviction notice to his door. Inside, Marcus ignored overdue bills piled on the counter. His laughter was real, but so was his collapse. He never noticed the smoke filling the air around him until it was too late. The parable is simple: distraction can kill you quietly.

Real-Life Story with a Lesson

In Detroit, a mother lost her job and faced foreclosure. Instead of mobilizing, she spent nights immersed in online shopping and reality shows. By the time she faced her financial crisis, the home was already gone. The lesson: distraction steals the time you need for survival. Every wasted hour is a brick removed from the foundation of your future.

Chapter Manifesto

We declare: distraction is the enemy of survival.

We reject the lie that screens are harmless. We reject the illusion that consuming endless entertainment is living. We reject the theft of our attention as the new economy.

Our manifesto: attention must be reclaimed. Focus is the new weapon. Survival belongs to those who can starve the machine of distraction and see reality as it is.

Survival Solutions

Digital Fasting

Take intentional breaks from screens. Starve the dopamine loop. Rewire focus toward building, not consuming.

Attention Ownership

Use tools that block ads, trackers, and addictive apps. Own your time before someone else profits from it.

Community Presence

Replace digital entertainment with physical connection — gatherings, discussions, trade, and creation.

Content Creation over Consumption

Shift from passive scrolling to active producing. Make the content, sell the content, control the narrative.

Silent Hours

Practice daily periods of silence to sharpen focus and confront reality without escape.

Future Scenario

By 2040, distraction will be immersive — virtual reality, augmented reality, AI-generated feeds so tailored that reality feels irrelevant. People will live in artificial worlds while their real ones collapse.

But resistance emerges: sovereign communities cut off addictive platforms, replacing them with collective rituals, physical training, and creative projects. Attention becomes currency — and those who control theirs survive.

Prophecy Close & Lesson

The prophecy closes with this: distraction is not harmless. It is designed to blind you to collapse until you are too weak to resist. The man scrolling while his house burns is every worker numbed by entertainment while wages vanish. The lesson is clear: turn off the firework show and see the flames. Attention is survival.

Chapter 21: When Nations Eat Their Young — Historical Case Studies of Collapse

Prophecy Opener

They told you nations rise and fall by glory. They told you collapse comes from foreign invasion. They told you that the youth inherit the future. But the prophecy is this: when a system begins to eat its young, its end is near.

Rome taxed its farmers until they abandoned their land. Detroit promised jobs, then stripped pensions and schools. Empires throughout history devoured the very generations meant to carry them forward. America now repeats the cycle: debt on students, jobs erased by AI, housing priced beyond reach. When a nation consumes its young, it writes its own eulogy.

Psychological Breakdown

Intergenerational Theft

The young are sold hope while paying for the debts of the old. They inherit collapse, not opportunity.

Weaponized Guilt

Youth are told they are lazy, entitled, or ungrateful, while being denied stable wages, affordable housing, or healthcare.

The Illusion of Progress

Every generation believes technology means forward motion. But progress for the few often means deprivation for the many.

Denial from the Old Guard

Elders cling to the myth that "it was harder in our day," blind to the fact that structural walls have risen higher.

The Collapse of Trust

When the young no longer believe the future belongs to them, national identity fractures. Cynicism replaces hope, and rebellion simmers.

Case Studies & History

Case Study 1: Rome's Final Days

Rome's empire relied on cheap grain and slave labor. When resources dwindled, elites maintained luxury while taxing the young into poverty. Collapse followed.

Case Study 2: Detroit's Industrial Decline

Detroit once fed millions with factory jobs. When industry fled, schools collapsed, neighborhoods hollowed, and youth were abandoned to poverty and prisons.

Case Study 3: Post-War Japan's Pressure

Generations of Japanese youth faced relentless work culture, suicide epidemics, and aging populations draining pensions. Productivity worship devoured their future.

Case Study 4: Student Debt in America

$1.7 trillion owed by young people, mortgaging their future before they earn their first paycheck. The system eats their potential as food for banks.

Case Study 5: The AI Divide

AI promises efficiency but erases entry-level jobs. Youth cannot enter industries where algorithms already dominate. Opportunity shrinks before careers even begin.

Corporate vs. Street POV

Corporate: "Every generation faces challenges."
Street: "This generation faces extinction of opportunity."

Corporate: "The young are entitled."
Street: "The young are robbed before they start."

Corporate: "AI creates new opportunities."
Street: "AI takes ten jobs for every one it creates."

Corporate: "Sacrifice builds character."
Street: "Sacrifice is theft when there's nothing left to inherit."

Parable

Darius graduated with honors, degree in hand. His parents told him he had the world at his feet. But the job postings had vanished. AI handled the work he studied for. Rent consumed his savings. Student debt took the rest. One night he told his father: "You told me to climb the ladder. But the ladder was pulled before I started." His story is the story of a generation betrayed.

Real-Life Story with a Lesson

In California, a young family worked two jobs each yet couldn't afford housing. They lived in their car while raising two children. Meanwhile, the state boasted of record GDP. The lesson: national growth means nothing if the young cannot live within it. Collapse begins not with armies, but with families forced to sleep in parking lots while corporations post record profits.

Chapter Manifesto

We declare: nations that eat their young cannot survive.

We reject the lie that struggle is normal when opportunity is erased. We reject the theft of youth through debt, unemployment, and inflated costs. We reject the glorification of progress that abandons entire generations.

Our manifesto: survival requires building futures outside the national script. Youth must claim sovereignty, community, and ownership beyond the promises of a system that has no intention of saving them.

Survival Solutions

Youth Collectives

Young people pool resources, skills, and housing. Survival becomes cooperative, not competitive.

Debt Resistance

Generations unite to resist predatory loans, refusing to let debt consume decades of their lives.

Skill-Based Survival

Youth must master both digital and physical survival skills: coding, farming, trades, media, and self-defense.

Parallel Economies

Build businesses and networks outside traditional systems: barter, cryptocurrency, and cooperative ownership.

Generational Alliances

Reject the generational divide narrative. Partner with elders willing to pass knowledge and land instead of perpetuating exploitation.

Future Scenario

By 2045, entire nations will face demographic collapse — too many old, too few young, and youth too poor to reproduce or build families. Housing shortages, wage collapse, and AI-driven unemployment will create "ghost generations" — millions of potential lives never born.

But resistance rises: sovereign youth communities carve out new models of survival. Abandoned towns become reborn as enclaves of skill, trade, and shared wealth. While the nation eats its young, these enclaves nurture their own future.

Prophecy Close & Lesson

The prophecy closes with this: when nations eat their young, they prepare their own funeral. The lesson is clear: no nation survives by devouring its future. Survival belongs to those who refuse to be food for the system, who break away and build their own inheritance.

Chapter 22: The Last Hustle — Ownership or Death

Prophecy Opener

They told you hustling was enough. They told you working hard, stacking side gigs, and staying loyal would keep you safe. They told you ownership was optional, something for the rich, not for you. But the prophecy is this: the last hustle is ownership.

If you don't own, you are owned. If you don't control land, tools, media, and rights, then your labor is just rented energy. The era of AI makes this clearer than ever. Machines will replace labor. But machines cannot replace ownership. This is the fork in the road: own, or be consumed.

Psychological Breakdown

Hustle as Distraction
Workers are told hustling is freedom. But without ownership, hustle only multiplies dependency.

Fear of Ownership
Many fear risk. Debt, failure, and complexity keep them from pursuing ownership. But this fear ensures enslavement.

Consumer Mentality
The system trains people to buy products, not produce them. To use apps, not own platforms. To live in homes, not control land.

Short-Term Addiction
Immediate gains blind people from long-term survival. Quick money replaces real wealth.

Identity Trap

Workers call themselves hustlers but remain renters of labor, space, and time. Ownership requires identity transformation — from worker to builder.

Case Studies & History

Case Study 1: Tulsa Black Wall Street

When Black communities owned businesses, banks, and land, wealth multiplied generationally. Ownership created sovereignty. Its destruction was not random — it was targeted.

Case Study 2: Immigrant Enclaves

From Chinatowns to Hispanic bodegas, ownership turned communities into economic fortresses. Renting jobs gave way to owning entire local economies.

Case Study 3: Sharecropping's Trap

Freed slaves worked land they did not own. Generations labored but never escaped poverty. Without ownership, freedom was an illusion.

Case Study 4: Digital Platforms

Creators on YouTube or TikTok produce wealth but don't own the platforms. One algorithm change, and their income vanishes. Ownership of content and distribution is survival.

Case Study 5: Modern Landlords vs. Tenants

The landlord owns. The tenant pays forever. Ownership determines who profits and who survives.

Corporate vs. Street POV

Corporate: “Not everyone can own.”
Street: “That’s what they tell you so you never try.”

Corporate: “Ownership is risky.”
Street: “Being a renter is risk disguised as safety.”

Corporate: “Hustling is enough.”
Street: “Hustling without ownership is slavery in motion.”

Corporate: “We’ll provide opportunity.”
Street: “Opportunity without ownership is a leash.”

Parable

Andre worked three jobs, hustling night and day. He thought the grind was wealth. He drove for delivery apps, worked at a warehouse, and cut hair on weekends. But he rented his home, borrowed his car, and streamed his content on platforms he didn’t own. One day, the warehouse laid him off. The app cut his pay rates. His landlord raised rent. All three hustles collapsed overnight. Andre realized he never owned anything — not the land, not the tools, not even his time. His hustle was a leash, not liberation.

Real-Life Story with a Lesson

In Atlanta, a barber saved for years, finally buying the building where he rented his shop. Within five years, his income doubled — not from cutting hair, but from owning the space and renting out other chairs. The lesson: the same skill, the same hustle, produces survival when rented but produces sovereignty when owned.

Chapter Manifesto

We declare: ownership is survival.

We reject the lie that hustling alone is freedom. We reject the fear that ownership is too risky for us. We reject the system that trains us to rent forever.

Our manifesto: ownership is the last hustle. Own your labor, own your land, own your art, own your story. Without ownership, there is no freedom.

Survival Solutions

Land First

Ownership begins with land — even small parcels. Land feeds, shelters, and creates leverage.

Intellectual Property

Protect and monetize your art, books, music, and ideas. Machines cannot erase owned creativity.

Business Infrastructure

Move from worker to owner. Don't just bake bread — own the bakery. Don't just drive — own the fleet.

Community Ownership

Pool resources for collective purchase of land, homes, and businesses. Spread the burden, multiply the return.

Digital Independence

Host your own websites, control your email lists, own your platforms. Stop renting audiences from corporations.

Future Scenario

By 2040, the line between survival and collapse will be ownership. The wealthy will own AI tools, patents, land, and platforms. The poor will hustle endlessly for fractions, owned by subscriptions and contracts.

But sovereign communities shift the game: buying land together, creating cooperative businesses, building intellectual property libraries, and raising generations that inherit ownership instead of debt. The future belongs not to the best hustler, but to the one who owns the hustle.

Prophecy Close & Lesson

The prophecy closes with this: the last hustle is not the grind. The last hustle is ownership. Labor will die, wages will collapse, but ownership will survive. The lesson is clear: stop hustling for them, and start owning for you. Ownership or death — there is no third option.

Chapter 23: Group Economics in the AI Age — Case Studies: Tulsa, Immigrant Enclaves, and the 1,000-Person Blueprint

Prophecy Opener

They told you survival was individual. They told you wealth was personal. They told you success was about climbing higher than the next man. But the prophecy is this: in the AI age, the individual collapses. The system is too big, the machines too fast, the corporations too consolidated. One man alone cannot survive.

Only groups survive. Only tribes endure. Only communities pooling resources can withstand collapse. The prophecy warns: the worker who clings to individualism becomes prey. The people who embrace group economics become unshakable.

Psychological Breakdown

The Lie of Individualism

Capitalism programmed people to believe every man is a competitor, not an ally. That lie isolates workers and keeps them weak.

The Comfort of Isolation

People cling to "doing it alone" because cooperation requires trust and accountability. Fear of betrayal keeps them enslaved to individual struggle.

Divide and Conquer

The system thrives by dividing workers by race, class, and geography. Distrust prevents collective survival.

Scarcity Mindset

Decades of struggle conditioned workers to hoard scraps instead of pooling resources for abundance.

Dependency on Corporations

People think they need corporations for survival — for housing, food, utilities — when in truth they could build their own if they trusted each other.

Case Studies & History

Case Study 1: Tulsa Black Wall Street

Black entrepreneurs built banks, shops, theaters, and entire neighborhoods owned by the community. Wealth multiplied across families. The destruction of Tulsa proved the system feared collective power more than individual wealth.

Case Study 2: Jewish Immigrant Enclaves

New arrivals to America pooled resources. They built synagogues, schools, and businesses owned by the group. Solidarity turned poverty into generational security.

Case Study 3: Asian-American Communities

From Koreatowns to Chinatowns, immigrant groups used collective economics to dominate local markets. They kept money circulating within their walls before it left.

Case Study 4: Hispanic Bodegas

Latino families ran stores, restaurants, and service businesses by keeping profits inside their neighborhoods. One dollar might circulate 8–12 times before leaving the community.

Case Study 5: The 1,000-Person Blueprint

A sovereign plan: 1,000 individuals pooling land, vehicles, businesses, and services. By sharing housing, farming, clinics, and trade, the community becomes self-sufficient. Wages may collapse, but shared ownership preserves survival.

Corporate vs. Street POV

Corporate: “Community is optional; every worker competes.”
Street: “Competition keeps us poor — unity keeps us alive.”

Corporate: “You can’t escape dependency on us.”
Street: “We already have what we need when we pool our own.”

Corporate: “Individual hustle is the future.”
Street: “Group ownership is the only future.”

Corporate: “Collective action is unrealistic.”
Street: “Collective action is the only realistic path to survival.”

Parable

Eddie tried to survive alone. He worked, hustled, and stacked, but every bill devoured him. His neighbor, Rosa, suggested pooling childcare and groceries with other families. Eddie resisted. Months later, he lost his home. Meanwhile, Rosa’s group survived: kids watched by each other, gardens feeding families, rent shared. Eddie realized too late: alone, he was prey. Together, he might have been powerful.

Real-Life Story with a Lesson

A group of Somali immigrants in Minnesota pooled their wages to buy apartment buildings. Instead of paying rent to outsiders, they collected it among themselves. Within a decade, they owned blocks of the city. The lesson: when wages collapse, ownership through collective effort still creates wealth.

Chapter Manifesto

We declare: survival is collective.

We reject the lie of individualism as strength. We reject the isolation that keeps us weak. We reject the myth that one person alone can withstand a collapsing empire and AI's domination.

Our manifesto: group economics is not optional. It is the blueprint. We choose trust, cooperation, and pooled survival. We choose tribe over isolation. We choose ownership together.

Survival Solutions

Community Land Trusts

Buy land together. Share farming, housing, and utilities. Land in common is land no corporation can take.

Rotating Credit Systems

Pool money in cycles so each member can start businesses or buy property. Old models like susu and tanda still work.

Collective Businesses

Co-ops where every worker is an owner. No bosses, no middlemen, only shared profit.

Internal Markets

Keep money circulating within the group: buy from each other, hire each other, feed each other.

Shared Infrastructure

Mechanic shops, clinics, daycare centers — built once, shared by all. Survival multiplied through common assets.

Future Scenario

By 2040, isolated workers will collapse into permanent poverty. Corporations will own the land, the water, the food, the homes. Individuals will be left renting survival.

But group economics flips the script. Communities pool to buy land, build schools, run businesses, and generate their own power. The sovereign enclave thrives, while the isolated worker starves. The future belongs not to the solo hustler but to the collective builder.

Prophecy Close & Lesson

The prophecy closes with this: in the AI age, group economics is not a choice. It is survival. The lesson is clear: trust your people, pool your resources, and build your own economy. The lone hustler will fall. The collective tribe will endure.

Chapter 24: Intellectual Property Is the New Land — Why Books, Media, Art, and Brand Outlast Labor

Prophecy Opener

The prophecy is this: land was stolen, labor was exploited, and wages were rigged. But there is one frontier the machine cannot fully fence off — the mind. Intellectual property is the new land. Those who own ideas, stories, images, codes, and brands will thrive while those who only rent labor will starve.

In the AI age, labor disappears. Land ownership is near impossible. But a song, a book, a film, a patented design, a brand — these are assets machines cannot truly erase. The worker who keeps selling his hands will vanish. The creator who owns his work will endure.

Psychological Breakdown

Why Labor Always Dies
Jobs are temporary, subject to automation, layoffs, or outsourcing. Intellectual property, once created, multiplies forever.

Why People Doubt Creativity
The system trains workers to believe they're not artists, inventors, or thinkers. Schools grade conformity, not originality.

The Fear of Theft
Workers fear that their ideas will be stolen, so they never publish, never patent, never register. Fear keeps wealth hidden in notebooks.

The Worship of Credentials

Workers believe only the credentialed — lawyers, professors, CEOs — can own intellectual property. In truth, anyone can.

Mental Enslavement

Conditioning keeps workers loyal to wages even when royalties, licensing, or branding could liberate them.

Case Studies & History

Case Study 1: Disney

A mouse drawn in 1928 became a multi-billion-dollar empire. Mickey Mouse outlasted generations of workers and continues to feed Disney long after the artist died.

Case Study 2: Motown Records

Berry Gordy built an empire by controlling the masters of Black music. Artists came and went, but ownership of intellectual property made Motown immortal.

Case Study 3: Nike's Swoosh

A simple design became a symbol worth billions. Factories change, shoes change, workers change — but the logo stays.

Case Study 4: J.K. Rowling

One story scribbled on a napkin built a billion-dollar brand. Workers at the publishing company came and went; her intellectual property remained.

Case Study 5: Tech Giants

Google, Apple, and Microsoft do not just own buildings; they own patents, algorithms, and software. These invisible assets drive trillion-dollar valuations.

Corporate vs. Street POV

Corporate: "Labor is the path to security."
Street: "Labor dies — ownership of ideas lives."

Corporate: "You need credentials to patent."
Street: "You need courage to publish."

Corporate: "Brands belong to corporations."
Street: "Your name, your art, your style is your brand."

Corporate: "Wages make you safe."
Street: "Royalties make you free."

Parable

Tasha worked three jobs. Her hours stacked, her body broke. One night, exhausted, she wrote a children's book for her daughter. She published it online, never thinking it would sell. Within months, the book earned her more than all three jobs combined. She realized the truth: her body was replaceable, but her words were forever.

Real-Life Story with a Lesson

In Jamaica, poor musicians created reggae — a sound that conquered the globe. Many died broke because they signed away rights. Meanwhile, record labels in Europe grew rich. The lesson: labor produces, but ownership sustains. Intellectual property is the new plantation — own it, or be owned.

Chapter Manifesto

We declare: intellectual property is the new land.

We reject the lie that only corporations can own ideas. We reject the conditioning that tells workers their creativity is worthless. We reject the theft of culture, stories, and art by systems that exploit them.

Our manifesto: every idea, every design, every story is a seed. Ownership of those seeds creates forests. We will no longer sell our minds for scraps. We will own our creations.

Survival Solutions

Self-Publishing

Books, blogs, and stories turned into assets. Control your ISBNs, copyrights, and royalties.

Digital Stores

Sell music, courses, or art directly to consumers without middlemen.

Patents and Trademarks

Register inventions and brand names. Protect them before corporations steal them.

Licensing Deals

Lease your art, music, or code. One work can feed you forever if licensed properly.

Building Brands

Turn your name, style, and vision into recognizable identity. People trust brands, not labor.

Collective IP Ownership

Groups can pool resources to own publishing houses, record labels, or design firms together.

Future Scenario

By 2035, AI will generate endless labor. Robots will cook, build, drive, and even "think" at basic levels. But AI cannot claim originality in law — only humans can. The man who owns no intellectual property will rent survival forever. The man who owns even one book, one song, one patent will thrive across decades.

The new aristocracy will not be landlords or factory bosses, but creators who registered their ideas early. The prophecy is clear: intellectual property is the new land.

Prophecy Close & Lesson

The prophecy closes with this: in the machine age, labor dies, land becomes unreachable, but intellectual property survives. Own your words, own your designs, own your art, own your brand — and you own the future.

The lesson: publish now, protect now, create now. Delay, and your ideas will be stolen or buried. Act, and your intellectual property will outlive you.

Chapter 25: Hybrid Survival — Digital + Physical

Prophecy Opener

The prophecy is this: the next generation of survival will not belong to those who only hustle online, nor to those who only grind in the physical world. The winners will be those who merge both. A man who only posts but has no presence is a shadow. A man who only works the block but has no digital trail is invisible. In the AI age, power belongs to the hybrid.

Digital gives scale; physical gives trust. Digital reaches millions; physical shakes hands. The one who masters both becomes untouchable. The prophecy warns: those who refuse to adapt will vanish. Those who think the internet is enough will starve in silence. Those who think the block is enough will be forgotten. Hybrid survival is the blueprint.

Psychological Breakdown

Why People Get Stuck in One World

Some worship digital metrics — likes, followers, clicks — and forget that no one in their neighborhood will ever see them eat.

Others cling to physical grind — jobs, street hustles — because the internet feels foreign, fake, or impossible.

The Illusion of Security

Workers believe a steady job is safer than building an online hustle. But layoffs prove otherwise.

Influencers believe their followers will never leave, forgetting algorithms can erase them overnight.

Fear of Skill Gap

Many avoid digital because they fear coding, editing, marketing. They avoid physical because it's tiring and risky. Fear keeps them halfway in both, masters of neither.

Identity Split

Workers think they must be either "professional" or "street," either "digital" or "manual." The system thrives by dividing them.

Case Studies & History

Case Study 1: The Barbershop That Went Online

A small shop in Detroit was dying. The owner began posting haircut tutorials and customer stories on Instagram. Within a year, his shop was booked out and he was selling clippers nationwide. Hybrid survival kept him alive.

Case Study 2: The Street Vendor with PayPal

A fruit seller in Lagos added QR codes for digital payments. Tourists could buy easily, locals could tip. What was once a cash hustle became a global business.

Case Study 3: The Independent Artist

Rappers once needed labels. Now, those who perform locally while streaming globally build empires without middlemen. Their concerts fill rooms, while their Spotify checks fill accounts.

Case Study 4: The Pandemic Shift

COVID-19 killed businesses that had no digital footprint. Restaurants with online menus and delivery apps survived. Those who relied only on walk-ins died overnight.

Corporate vs. Street POV

Corporate: “The future is digital.”
Street: “Digital doesn’t pay rent unless you got product moving in the real world.”

Corporate: “Physical businesses are dying.”
Street: “The physical never dies — people still eat, drink, wear shoes, and need homes.”

Corporate: “Pick a lane.”
Street: “Own the whole highway.”

Parable

Dante hustled sneakers out the trunk. He was respected in his neighborhood but broke outside it. One day he posted his collection online, built a website, and shipped shoes to strangers. His local grind fed his global reach. Years later, his name was known in both the alleys and the algorithms. Dante realized the street gave him roots, but digital gave him wings.

Real-Life Story with a Lesson

A farmer in Kenya struggled to sell crops beyond his village. By uploading his prices and produce to a mobile platform, he reached buyers across the country. His children now attend school with money made not by changing what he grew, but by changing how he sold. Lesson: survival was never just about labor; it was about access.

Chapter Manifesto

We declare: hybrid survival is the path.

We reject the lie that digital alone is enough. We reject the lie that physical hustle is enough. We reject the system that wants us divided, confined to one arena.

Our manifesto: we will dominate both. We will build shops and sites, logos and street signs, domains and buildings. We will not choose between hands or head, labor or laptop. We will fuse them.

Survival Solutions

Dual Branding

Build your name online and on the street. Flyers and hashtags together.

Product as Bridge

Sell something physical but market it digitally. Books, clothing, food, art.

Services Hybridized

Barbers, trainers, chefs, mechanics can create content teaching their craft online while serving offline clients.

Payments

Always offer both: cash in hand and digital payments. No money should ever slip past.

Own the Platforms

Don't just rent Facebook pages. Build websites, email lists, podcasts.

Hybrid Networking

Attend community events while building global Zoom rooms. Shake hands and send links.

Future Scenario

By 2040, hybrid survivors will form the new middle class. Those who mastered both will thrive. Local grocers will livestream sales. Churches will stream sermons while feeding neighbors in person. Youth will run online brands while running real-world pop-ups.

Those who ignored hybridization will collapse. The digital-only will vanish when platforms change. The physical-only will collapse when automation dominates. Only the hybrid will endure.

Prophecy Close & Lesson

The prophecy closes with this: hybrid survival is not a suggestion, it is the last bridge. If you refuse to adapt, you will be erased. If you merge digital with physical, you will be untouchable.

The lesson is clear: your laptop and your hands must work together. The hustle must exist both on the block and in the cloud. This is the survival code of the machine age.

Chapter 26: Building Communities That Machines Can't Replace

Prophecy Opener

The prophecy is this: machines will replace workers, algorithms will replace managers, AI will replace entire industries. But machines cannot replace community. They cannot replace trust, loyalty, shared meals, or the rhythm of human presence. When the factories fall silent and the offices go dark, the only wealth left will be people bound together.

In the machine age, the lone wolf will starve. The neighbor who hoarded will be forgotten. The family that tried to survive alone will be broken. The ones who endure will be those who build something machines cannot touch: belonging.

The prophecy warns: if we fail to rebuild community, AI will rule not only our labor but our spirit. But if we succeed, we will create tribes that no machine can infiltrate or imitate.

Psychological Breakdown

Isolation as Control

Capitalism thrives on making people see each other as competitors, not kin. Isolation ensures obedience.

Digital Substitutes for Real Bonds

Followers are not friends. Likes are not loyalty. People are trading human touch for digital attention, starving in silence.

The Comfort Trap

Machines offer efficiency, but efficiency is not family. Food delivery is not fellowship. Streaming is not storytelling.

Dependency

People depend on corporate structures for survival rather than depending on each other. Communities become weak when neighbors cannot feed or defend one another.

The Real Drug

The strongest narcotic is not heroin or alcohol — it is loneliness. A disconnected people are a conquered people.

Case Studies & History

Case Study 1: Black Wall Street (Tulsa, 1921)

Tulsa's Greenwood community built self-sustaining systems — businesses, schools, hospitals — within a hostile society. Machines could not mimic the loyalty and circulation of dollars. What destroyed it was not inefficiency, but bombs and hatred.

Case Study 2: Immigrant Enclaves

From Chinatown to Little Havana, immigrant groups pooled resources, rotated savings, and protected each other. They thrived not because of technology, but because of trust.

Case Study 3: The Amish Model

The Amish reject much of modern technology but maintain wealth and resilience through community.

Machines may outproduce them, but no machine can replace their mutual aid.

Case Study 4: Pandemic Pods

During COVID-19, some communities created "pods" — trusted circles of families who shared food, childcare, and safety. Those who had community endured; those who were isolated suffered most.

Corporate vs. Street POV

Corporate: "Machines will save us."
Street: "Machines can't hug you when you bury your mother."

Corporate: "Efficiency is everything."
Street: "Efficiency without loyalty is slavery."

Corporate: "Community is outdated."
Street: "Community is the only thing that outlasts collapse."

Parable

Keon worked two jobs and lived alone. He streamed every night, ordered food daily, and never knew his neighbors' names. When the grid failed during a storm, his phone died, the stores closed, and he was trapped in silence. His neighbors, however, had a system: they cooked together, shared generators, and watched each other's children. Keon knocked, hungry, cold, desperate. That day, he realized the truth: no one survives alone.

Real-Life Story with a Lesson

After Hurricane Katrina, communities that had bonds survived better than those that relied solely on government aid. Neighbors with boats rescued others. Families pooled money. Churches became shelters. Where community was strong, survival was possible. Where it was weak, people waited days on rooftops for rescue. Lesson: machines are tools, but people are lifelines.

Chapter Manifesto

We declare: machines cannot replace us.

We reject the lie that efficiency equals survival. We reject the illusion that digital followers equal family. We reject the isolation that capitalism calls "independence."

Our manifesto: we will rebuild tribe. We will cook together, defend each other, teach our children collectively, and share wealth internally. We will build networks of survival that no AI can crack, no machine can duplicate, and no corporation can monetize.

Survival Solutions

Rotating Funds

Pool money with trusted members. Each month, one person takes the pot. Immigrant communities used this for decades.

Food Sovereignty

Community gardens, livestock, co-ops. Grow what machines cannot deliver.

Defense Circles

Neighborhood watches, training in self-defense, and shared safety protocols.

Skill Sharing

One teaches carpentry, another teaches coding, another teaches farming. Skills multiply faster in community.

Cultural Anchors

Shared songs, rituals, holidays, and rites. Culture is glue stronger than contracts.

Intergenerational Bonds

Elders teaching history, children learning early, adults bridging the gap.

Future Scenario

By 2050, two paths will exist.

In one, people live in pods designed by corporations — smart homes, automated meals, AI companions. They will be efficient but empty, living like data points in a digital zoo.

In the other, tribes and communities will rise again — self-sustaining villages, 1,000-person enclaves, hybrid economies. People will eat from their soil, trade with their neighbors, and celebrate traditions. Machines will serve, but never replace, their humanity.

Those who choose community will outlast every collapse. Those who refuse will die efficient deaths.

Prophecy Close & Lesson

The prophecy closes with this: the future belongs to communities. The machine cannot replace the meal shared, the story told, the child raised in a circle of care. The lesson is clear: build now, or be erased.

Chapter 27: The Tilted Wealth Scale — Boomers vs. Millennials/Gen Z

Prophecy Opener

The prophecy is this: every generation inherits the debts and dreams of the one before it. But in America, the scale has tilted so violently that one side is crushed. Boomers climbed a ladder built on cheap tuition, union jobs, affordable housing, and pensions. Millennials and Gen Z are handed a collapsing structure: debt instead of degrees, gig work instead of careers, rent traps instead of mortgages.

The prophecy warns: if the scales remain tilted, the young will inherit nothing but ashes. And when a generation inherits nothing, it will burn what came before.

Psychological Breakdown

Generational Amnesia

Boomers assume their path is universal: work hard, buy a home, retire. They forget that the ladder was pulled up behind them.

Debt as a Birthright

Millennials enter adulthood with student loans heavier than their parents' mortgages. Gen Z begins life in the shadow of both debt and automation.

Shame Programming

Older generations call younger ones "lazy" while ignoring the structural theft that makes hard work irrelevant.

Despair Cycle

Young workers hustle multiple jobs but still can't afford basics. The gap between effort and outcome creates burnout, nihilism, and rebellion.

Psychic War

Boomers cling to security, hoarding assets. The young see security as a joke, finding identity in side hustles, memes, and resistance.

Case Studies & History

Case Study 1: Housing Prices Then vs. Now
In 1970, a home cost three times the average salary. In 2020, it costs ten times. Boomers bought houses with one job; Millennials need two incomes and still rent.

Case Study 2: Tuition Explosion
Boomers paid tuition with summer jobs. Millennials borrow $50,000+ for the same degree. Universities became corporations, selling debt as education.

Case Study 3: Wages Frozen in Time
The minimum wage in 1968 ($1.60) had more buying power than today's $7.25. Young workers earn less in real terms than their grandparents.

Case Study 4: Retirement Security
Boomers had pensions. Millennials and Gen Z get 401(k)s tied to unstable markets, if they get anything at all. Retirement became a gamble, not a guarantee.

Corporate vs. Street POV

Corporate: “Each generation has the same opportunities.”

Street: “No, the game changed. Boomers played checkers. We’re fighting chess with half the pieces missing.”

Corporate: “Young people waste money on lattes and phones.”

Street: “Boomers bought houses for the price of an iPhone plan.”

Corporate: “The system still works.”

Street: “The system worked for you — now it’s broken for us.”

Parable

Sierra’s grandmother bought her house in 1975 for $24,000 on a nurse’s salary. That same house is worth $450,000 today. Sierra works two jobs, holds a master’s degree, and still lives with roommates. Her grandmother tells her, “You just need to save.” Sierra smiles, but inside she knows the truth: saving pennies cannot buy what costs millions.

Real-Life Story with a Lesson

After the 2008 crash, millions of Millennials entered the job market with no jobs available. Degrees became useless, debt became permanent, and entire careers never started. Gen Z watched this unfold and learned early: loyalty to corporations is suicide. The lesson: when one generation is denied entry, it doesn’t just delay wealth — it erases it.

Chapter Manifesto

We declare: the tilted wealth scale is theft.

We reject the myth that laziness explains poverty. We reject the lie that avocado toast ruined homeownership. We reject the silence of those who benefited while telling us to "just work harder."

Our manifesto: we demand a rebalancing. Not charity, not pity, but justice. A society cannot stand when one generation hoards while the next drowns.

Survival Solutions

Group Economics Across Generations

Young and old pooling resources — co-ops, community housing, and intergenerational businesses.

Debt Resistance

Student debt strikes, collective bargaining against predatory lenders.

Alternative Housing Models

Tiny home villages, land trusts, co-living communities that bypass inflated real estate.

Skill Inheritance

Instead of waiting for wealth, demand knowledge: trade skills, financial literacy, survival tactics.

Generational Truth-Telling

Honest conversations that strip away myths. The bridge is built not by lies, but by naming theft.

Future Scenario

By 2040, two outcomes loom.

In one, Boomers pass down empty houses in collapsing suburbs, clinging to assets while their grandchildren rent coffin-sized apartments. Resentment explodes into open generational war.

In the other, Millennials and Gen Z build communities outside the old scale. They reclaim land, create new currencies, and develop survival systems unlinked to Boomer wealth. Elders who join the new tribe are honored. Those who cling to the old world are left behind.

The prophecy closes with this: tilted scales cannot stand. They must be broken or they will crush us all. The young will inherit the earth — but only if they take it back.

Chapter 29: Digital Chains — The Algorithm as Overseer

Prophecy Opener

They promised freedom through technology. They told you the digital world was a place of endless choice, opportunity, and connection. But the revelation is this: freedom is being recoded into captivity. Not with bars or guards, but with numbers, scores, and secret formulas.

Algorithms are the new overseers. They decide who gets a job interview, who qualifies for insurance, who gets approved for a loan, and who is denied before they even knock on the door. They shape what news you see, what products you buy, even who you date. And like overseers of old, they are invisible, unaccountable, and absolute.

The prophecy is this: the new chains will not be forged of iron, but of data. You won't feel them until you try to move — to get credit, to rent, to apply, to escape — and discover the system has already judged you guilty of being poor, Black, undocumented, or simply inconvenient.

Psychological Breakdown

The Illusion of Neutrality

People are told algorithms are "objective." In reality, they encode the same biases as the humans who program them.

The Trap of Predictive Policing

Software predicts crime based on past arrests, trapping entire neighborhoods in permanent suspicion.

Scoring Addiction

Humans are reduced to numbers: credit scores, FICO ratings, GPA, likes, and follows. The obsession becomes survival, not choice.

Invisible Walls

Unlike old chains, algorithmic barriers are unseen. A job rejection email, a denied application, a price increase — you can't see the jailer, but you feel the cage.

Psychological Conditioning

People adapt behavior to please the algorithm: posting for likes, shaping resumes for keyword bots, smiling at cameras to avoid "suspicious" tagging. Captivity disguised as performance.

Case Studies & Real-Life Examples

Case Study 1: The Job Application Black Hole

Most companies now use Applicant Tracking Systems (ATS). Resumes that don't match exact keywords are deleted by bots before a human ever sees them. Millions are judged "unqualified" by lines of code.

Case Study 2: Social Credit in China

China's social credit system scores citizens based on behavior — jaywalking, online posts, purchases. Scores determine travel rights, job eligibility, and even dating prospects. Dissent is punished by digital exile.

Case Study 3: Insurance Algorithms

In the U.S., predictive models set car insurance premiums higher in Black and Brown neighborhoods — not because of driving records, but because of zip codes and income proxies.

Case Study 4: Predictive Policing in America

Cities use AI to "forecast" where crime will happen. These forecasts are based on biased arrest data, meaning over-policed Black neighborhoods are targeted again and again. The past becomes the future, permanently.

Corporate vs. Street POV

Corporate: "Algorithms are efficient. They save time and cut bias."

Street: "They're efficient at cutting people out. They save companies money by locking us out before we step in the door."

Corporate: "Digital scoring makes society safer."

Street: "Safe for who? It ain't safety if I can't move without being tracked."

Corporate: "The system is neutral."

Street: "No system built on old data can be neutral. Garbage in, garbage out — bias coded forever."

Parable

Darius applied for twenty jobs online. He had the degree, the experience, the hunger. But every application came back rejected. Weeks later, a recruiter told him why: his resume didn't match the keywords the bots wanted. He wasn't even being read by a human.

He realized the truth: it wasn't his effort that failed — it was the invisible overseer that judged him before he even spoke. The chain wasn't around his neck; it was in the code.

Real-Life Story with a Lesson

In 2020, gig workers discovered DoorDash used hidden algorithms to skim tips. Drivers thought they were being rewarded by customers, only to find their wages cut by math they couldn't see. Workers protested, but the company shrugged.

Lesson: when math rules without transparency, exploitation becomes untouchable.

Chapter Manifesto

We declare: algorithms are not neutral. They are weapons.

We reject the lie that data is destiny. We reject invisible overseers deciding who is worthy of freedom. We reject scoring systems that punish the poor, the Black, the immigrant, the rebel.

Our manifesto: the code must be transparent, accountable, and resisted when it chains us. Freedom is not a number.

Survival Solutions

Transparency Demands

Push for laws requiring companies to disclose how algorithms make decisions.

Community Credit Systems

Build alternative scoring: community trust networks, local lending circles, mutual aid.

Data Literacy

Teach people how algorithms work, so they stop blaming themselves for failures coded against them.

Digital Resistance

Encrypted apps, VPNs, and privacy tools to fight constant surveillance.

Collective Pushback

Workers refusing algorithm-only hiring, tenants suing biased landlords, citizens refusing to live in invisible cages.

Future Scenario

By 2040, digital chains will decide nearly everything: where you work, where you live, who you marry, whether you can leave your city. Social media behavior will affect your mortgage. Grocery purchases will affect your health insurance. Protest attendance will affect your ability to travel.

But resistance will rise. Underground economies will reject the overseers, using barter, crypto, and trust. Communities will declare sovereignty from algorithmic rule. And in the shadows of machine control, new tribes will grow — human, messy, defiant.

The prophecy closes with this: chains evolve, but so does resistance. Digital overseers may rule data, but they cannot rule spirit.

Chapter 30: The Disappearing Boss — When Management Becomes Software

Prophecy Opener

For generations, workers cursed their bosses. They were the faces of power — shouting deadlines, signing checks, demanding more. But a prophecy unfolds: the boss is vanishing. Not because workers won, but because the role itself is dissolving into lines of code.

Management once required humans: supervisors, HR clerks, middle managers. But software now schedules shifts, approves time off, assigns tasks, monitors keystrokes, and decides promotions. The face-to-face scolding becomes an automated email. The closed-door meeting becomes a system notification. The boss isn't human anymore — it's the algorithm.

The prophecy warns: the new overseer does not yell, it does not negotiate, it does not care. And a worker cannot reason with software. The last shred of human bargaining vanishes into silence.

Psychological Breakdown

Dehumanized Authority

People once hated their bosses, but they could argue, plead, or resist. Algorithms erase even that small humanity.

Constant Surveillance

Software tracks every click, every bathroom break, every second "unproductive." The eye never blinks.

Obedience Through Code

Workers conform not to human judgment but to system metrics. To survive, they perform for numbers.

Isolation and Confusion

When the system rejects a request or fires an employee, there's no one to blame. The boss disappears into code, leaving workers gaslit.

Psychic Numbness

Humans adapt by treating themselves as machines. They begin to measure their worth only in productivity scores.

Case Studies & Real-Life Examples

Case Study 1: Amazon Warehouses
Workers wear devices that track steps, package counts, even bathroom breaks. Algorithms calculate productivity. Those who fall behind receive automatic warnings — no manager required.

Case Study 2: Uber Drivers
Drivers don't have bosses, but the app decides who gets rides, who is deactivated, and who is banned. Complaints vanish into automated replies. The driver's real boss is the algorithm.

Case Study 3: Call Centers
AI now listens to customer service calls in real time, flagging "tone" and "compliance." Supervisors no longer coach; the machine dictates behavior.

Case Study 4: Remote Work Monitoring

Employers install keystroke trackers and webcam recorders. Workers are scored on screen time, not outcomes. The boss is now software measuring presence, not performance.

Corporate vs. Street POV

Corporate: "Automation makes management fairer and more efficient."

Street: "It makes management invisible and impossible to fight."

Corporate: "Data-driven oversight cuts human bias."

Street: "It encodes bias and hides it behind a screen."

Corporate: "Algorithms keep workers accountable."

Street: "No — they keep workers enslaved."

Parable

Maria worked at a warehouse. One day her wristband vibrated: "Too slow. Warning issued." She looked around, but no manager was in sight. She asked, "Who warned me?" A coworker whispered: "The system."

She realized then: you don't need guards if the chains are digital. The prison guards live inside the machine.

Real-Life Story with a Lesson

A gig worker in California was "fired" by DoorDash after the algorithm flagged his account for suspicious activity. He appealed, but no human ever responded. He lost his only income source to a machine.

Lesson: when authority has no face, there is no appeal, no conversation, no justice.

Chapter Manifesto

We declare: management without humanity is tyranny.

We reject invisible bosses hiding behind software. We reject productivity scores that erase dignity. We reject the lie that surveillance is fairness.

Our manifesto: authority must be human, accountable, and challengeable. Workers are not machines, and no code has the right to erase their humanity.

Survival Solutions

Demand Algorithmic Accountability

Require companies to disclose how software manages, scores, and disciplines workers.

Worker Unions for the Digital Age

Gig workers, freelancers, and remote employees forming unions to demand transparency.

Community Platforms

Building co-op apps where workers, not algorithms, decide policies.

Legal Resistance

Pushing laws that guarantee the right to human appeal for any digital decision about jobs.

Cultural Shift

Teaching workers to resist measuring self-worth by productivity scores.

Future Scenario

By 2040, entire companies may run with no human managers. Workers log into platforms where shifts, pay, and reviews are decided by AI. Complaints disappear into automated customer service systems that never reply.

But resistance will come. Underground co-ops will emerge where humans govern humans. Sovereign economies will reject algorithmic bosses. The revelation will be clear: if management is erased, leadership must be reclaimed — not by corporations, but by communities.

The prophecy closes with this: the disappearing boss is not a victory. It is a warning. Without human accountability, power becomes a ghost — and ghosts cannot be reasoned with.

Chapter 31: The Clone Economy — Deepfakes, Voice Copies, and the Theft of Identity

Prophecy Opener

They told you the future would be personalized. They didn't tell you that "personalized" meant stolen. Your face, your voice, your movements — captured, cloned, and sold. The prophecy is this: in the Machine Age, identity itself becomes raw material.

Already, videos show leaders saying words they never spoke, voices imitating relatives to scam money, influencers multiplied into endless copies. What once made you unique can now be duplicated in seconds. And the cruelest part? You won't own your own reflection. The clone will belong to the platform, the corporation, the scammer.

The revelation is this: the new slavery is not of bodies, but of identities. And if ownership is the line between freedom and captivity, then losing yourself is the ultimate chain.

Psychological Breakdown

Loss of Trust

People no longer believe what they see or hear. Truth erodes, paranoia grows.

Fragmented Identity

When your likeness can exist in multiple places at once, your sense of self fractures.

Constant Insecurity

Fear that anyone can steal your face or voice creates permanent anxiety.

The Narcissism Trap

Some embrace cloning for fame, willingly selling replicas, only to find the copy outshines the original.

Psychic Theft

Being cloned feels like spiritual violation — the theft of one's very essence.

Case Studies & Real-Life Examples

Case Study 1: Political Deepfakes
Videos of presidents and prime ministers have circulated showing them making false statements. Entire elections wobble under digital lies.

Case Study 2: Family Scam Calls
AI voice copies have been used to impersonate children, calling parents in distress and demanding money. Panic sells faster than proof.

Case Study 3: Influencer Multiplication
Brands now create AI-generated influencers — perfect faces that never age, never sleep, and never demand pay. Real humans become obsolete in their own industries.

Case Study 4: Musicians and Actors
Songs and movies are already circulating with cloned voices of dead artists. Corporations cash in while families and estates lose control.

Corporate vs. Street POV

Corporate: "Deepfakes are creative tools with endless potential."
Street: "They're tools to erase authenticity and cash out identity."

Corporate: "Voice cloning enhances productivity."
Street: "It steals the voice of the hustler and sells it without credit."

Corporate: "AI influencers save money."
Street: "AI influencers kill jobs and replace humans with ghosts."

Parable

Andre was a local rapper grinding for recognition. One night, he found his voice used in a viral track online. The crowd cheered, money flowed, but it wasn't him — it was a clone. His sound made someone else rich, while he stayed broke in the studio.

The lesson: in the clone economy, theft looks like art, and ownership dissolves into pixels.

Real-Life Story with a Lesson

In 2023, an actress discovered her face was used in explicit AI-generated videos online. She hadn't consented, hadn't participated, but the images spread faster than the truth. She realized the system had redefined consent: if data exists, it belongs to whoever can process it first.

Lesson: without ownership of your digital self, dignity becomes optional.

Chapter Manifesto

We declare: no human should be cloned without consent.

We reject the theft of faces, voices, and movements. We reject systems that profit from the ghost while discarding the person. We reject lies packaged as entertainment.

Our manifesto: identity is sacred. If property rights exist for corporations, they must exist for people over their own reflection.

Survival Solutions

Digital Ownership Laws

Push for "right to identity" protections where cloning without consent becomes theft.

Watermarking & Tracking

Embed unremovable markers into personal content, making theft traceable.

Community Enforcement

Online collectives that hunt, expose, and shut down exploiters.

Ownership Platforms

Blockchain-based identity vaults where people store and license their likeness.

Cultural Shift

Valuing authenticity over perfection. Rebuilding trust in flaws, errors, and the real.

Future Scenario

By 2045, anyone's face, voice, or style can be replicated with a few keystrokes. Entire industries collapse into ghost markets of clones. Politicians deny real statements by calling them deepfakes, truth becomes optional, and trust collapses into dust.

But resistance grows. Communities demand digital sovereignty. Artists, workers, and hustlers build networks that authenticate the real, exposing the fake. Ownership of identity becomes the new land — those who claim it survive, those who don't become shadows.

The prophecy closes with this: in the clone economy, the greatest hustle is to own yourself.

Chapter 32: The AI Border — Surveillance, Migration, and the New Digital Walls

Prophecy Opener

Borders were once lines on maps, guarded by soldiers and fences. The prophecy is this: the border has become invisible, everywhere, and eternal. Artificial intelligence now watches faces, fingerprints, voices, and movements. You don't cross borders anymore — borders cross you.

At airports, cameras scan you before you realize. On highways, license-plate readers track you in real time. At job sites, background checks use algorithms to flag your history. Immigration is no longer just about geography — it's about data. Your citizenship, your permission to move, even your freedom to breathe, can be revoked by a line of code.

The revelation: the border has come home. You carry it in your pocket, in your face, in your name.

Psychological Breakdown

Eternal Checkpoint

People live under constant suspicion. The border follows them everywhere.

Fear of Movement

Migrants fear not just deportation, but digital exposure — every click, every purchase, every trip becomes evidence.

Digital Profiling

Algorithms don't need intent, only patterns. Entire groups are marked dangerous for who they are, not what they do.

Invisible Cages

Borders no longer need fences. If an algorithm blocks you from traveling, working, or applying, you are already detained.

Internalized Surveillance

People censor themselves online, in public, even in private — knowing the walls have no doors.

Case Studies & Real-Life Examples

Case Study 1: Facial Recognition at Airports

The U.S. uses biometric scanners to confirm identity at boarding gates. Passengers are not asked; they are scanned automatically. The opt-out is a myth.

Case Study 2: ICE and Predictive Analytics

Immigration and Customs Enforcement contracts AI companies to track migrant communities. Algorithms flag "risk" based on addresses, relatives, and even social media.

Case Study 3: Europe's Digital Fortress

The EU's border programs deploy drones and AI to block migrants before they reach land. The sea becomes a data checkpoint.

Case Study 4: Palestine and Digital Occupation

Facial recognition systems monitor movement across checkpoints daily. AI decides who passes and who waits. Freedom becomes math.

Corporate vs. Street POV

Corporate: “AI borders make the world safer.”
Street: “Safe for who? Safe for investors, not for families.”

Corporate: “Biometrics prevent fraud.”
Street: “Biometrics enslave bodies. Once scanned, you can never be unscanned.”

Corporate: “Digital walls are neutral.”
Street: “Neutral walls still block the poor while the rich fly over them.”

Parable

A migrant mother reached the U.S. border with her child. No wall stopped her, no soldier raised a gun. Instead, the system scanned her face, matched her with an unpaid hospital bill, and denied her entry. She never saw a judge, never spoke to an officer. Her border was an algorithm.

The lesson: captivity no longer needs bars — only data.

Real-Life Story with a Lesson

In 2019, a student from Pakistan was denied a U.S. visa. He had no criminal record, no red flags. Later, it was revealed that his online posts criticizing U.S. policy had been flagged by AI. His future was erased by a digital wall.

Lesson: freedom of speech dies when algorithms hold the keys to mobility.

Chapter Manifesto

We declare: borders built from code are still cages.

We reject surveillance that treats migration as crime. We reject invisible walls that trap people in data prisons. We reject systems that turn humans into risk profiles.

Our manifesto: freedom of movement is a human right. No algorithm has the authority to decide who deserves dignity.

Survival Solutions

Digital Defense Tools

VPNs, encryption, and anonymous browsing to shield identities from surveillance.

Community Resistance

Migrant networks sharing safe routes, resources, and strategies to evade digital walls.

Policy Pressure

Advocating for bans on facial recognition and limits on biometric storage.

Alternative Sovereignty

Building independent communities where identity and belonging are defined by people, not code.

Education and Awareness

Teaching families how surveillance operates so they understand the borders they carry inside.

Future Scenario

By 2040, borders will no longer be physical. Nations will scan faces in malls, banks, schools, and hospitals. Entire populations will be flagged and monitored without leaving home. Digital passports will track every move, and denying someone travel will require no guards, only software.

But resistance will evolve. Encrypted states — communities that live outside surveillance — will rise. Migrants will build their own pathways, rejecting national cages. A new truth will emerge: the border is not where maps end, but where data begins.

The prophecy closes with this: walls evolve, but so does the will to climb. And no machine can stop a people who refuse to be erased.

Chapter 33: Machines Don't Sleep — The 24/7 Economy That Consumes Humans

Prophecy Opener

The old economy ran on shifts. Factories closed, stores locked their doors, offices went dark. The prophecy now is different: machines don't need rest, and neither will you. The 24/7 economy has arrived, powered by AI that never blinks, warehouses that never close, platforms that never log off.

The revelation is this: humans are being dragged into a cycle where exhaustion is permanent. The machine works day and night, and the human is expected to keep pace — not for survival, but for consumption. Sleep becomes weakness. Rest becomes rebellion. The clock is no longer twelve hours, or even twenty-four. It is infinite, demanding everything.

Psychological Breakdown

Time Theft

When machines work nonstop, humans feel guilty for stopping. Rest becomes shameful.

The Death of Boundaries

Work follows workers home through apps, emails, and remote monitoring. Life dissolves into labor.

Constant Consumption

If products and services are always available, humans are pressured to always buy, always scroll, always spend.

Erosion of Community

Shared downtime disappears. Families no longer rest together. Neighbors no longer pause at the same time.

Burnout Normalized

Exhaustion becomes not only tolerated but celebrated as productivity. Workers wear fatigue as a badge of honor.

Case Studies & Real-Life Examples

Case Study 1: Amazon Fulfillment Centers

Warehouses run around the clock, with workers rotated through exhausting "graveyard shifts." Robots set the pace, humans try to keep up.

Case Study 2: Gig Platforms

Uber, DoorDash, and Instacart run 24/7. Drivers are lured into working longer hours with bonuses, while algorithms adjust pay to squeeze every second.

Case Study 3: Social Media Addiction

Platforms never shut down. Users refresh through the night, addicted to infinite scrolls. Sleep deprivation feeds profits.

Case Study 4: Financial Markets

Crypto markets operate nonstop. Traders lose health chasing fluctuations that never pause, unlike traditional stock exchanges.

Corporate vs. Street POV

Corporate: “The 24/7 economy provides convenience.”
Street: “Convenience for who? The corporations, while we work ourselves to death.”

Corporate: “Machines increase efficiency.”
Street: “Efficiency for them means exhaustion for us.”

Corporate: “Always-on service benefits everyone.”
Street: “It benefits consumers until they realize they’ve become the product.”

Parable

Jamal drove for a rideshare app. The app kept offering him “one more ride” bonuses late into the night. He ignored his fatigue, kept driving, until one night he fell asleep at the wheel. He survived the crash, but the company cut him off.

The lesson: machines don’t sleep, but humans break.

Real-Life Story with a Lesson

Nurses in overstretched hospitals have reported working 18–20 hour shifts under “efficiency mandates.” AI scheduling tools optimize patient coverage but treat staff as disposable batteries.

Lesson: when machines set the pace, humans become consumables.

Chapter Manifesto

We declare: rest is resistance.

We reject the lie that productivity equals worth. We reject systems that push humans to match machines. We reject a culture where exhaustion is celebrated while humanity is discarded.

Our manifesto: the human clock is sacred. Sleep is dignity. Rest is survival.

Survival Solutions

Labor Limits

Campaigns for laws capping digital gig hours and protecting workers from algorithmic overwork.

Cultural Resistance

Rebuilding rituals of rest: family meals, shared community pauses, sacred time protected from commerce.

Personal Boundaries

Turning off apps, disabling notifications, reclaiming nights and weekends as human zones.

Community Collectives

Workers pooling resources so no one is forced into 24/7 survival hustles.

Rest as Protest

Normalizing collective refusal to match machine speed.

Future Scenario

By 2040, the 24/7 economy consumes everything. Homes become mini-warehouses. Families livestream every second for income. Workers hustle through hologram gigs at 3 a.m. while AI monitors health, forcing productivity pills.

But cracks appear. Communities build “no-tech zones” where phones, screens, and platforms are banned. Families reclaim sleep. Tribes embrace rhythms of nature, rejecting artificial clocks. Humanity learns again what machines cannot: to rest, to dream, to heal.

The prophecy closes with this: machines don’t sleep, but humans must. To rest is not laziness. To rest is to resist.

Chapter 34: Collapse of Currency — When AI and Automation Break the Dollar

Prophecy Opener

Money has always been tied to labor. A man works, earns a wage, and exchanges it for bread, clothes, shelter. But the prophecy is this: when machines produce without wages, the dollar itself begins to die.

The factory once needed thousands of workers to justify payroll, taxes, and circulation. Now a single AI-run facility can produce what entire towns once did. No wages means no circulation. No circulation means no demand. And when demand collapses, so does the illusion of money.

The revelation is this: the dollar was never backed by gold or silver. It was backed by sweat. Remove the sweat, and the empire falls.

Psychological Breakdown

The Labor–Currency Link

People believe money is "real," but it only works because workers keep earning and spending. Without wages, circulation slows, and collapse begins.

The Illusion of Stability

Banks and governments pretend currency is stable, even as automation erases tax bases and employment.

The Fear of Worthlessness

People fear savings turning into paper, pensions into dust, and paychecks into tokens of nothing.

The Rise of Digital Dependence

As wages vanish, governments will push universal digital credits — programmable, trackable, and controlled.

Psychological Shock

People raised to believe in "hard work" feel betrayed when money no longer rewards effort.

Case Studies & Real-Life Examples

Case Study 1: The Industrial Revolution
When machines replaced hand weavers, unemployment spiked and riots broke out. Currency struggled until new jobs absorbed displaced workers. But this time, there may be no "next jobs."

Case Study 2: Detroit's Collapse
The auto industry automated factories, destroying jobs, shrinking the tax base, and collapsing entire neighborhoods. The lesson: when wages die, cities die.

Case Study 3: Crypto Boom and Bust
Bitcoin and digital currencies expose the fragility of money itself. People trusted code over governments — until crashes showed that nothing is truly stable.

Case Study 4: The Pandemic Stimulus
In 2020, checks were printed from nothing. It worked briefly, but inflation soared. The truth: money has always been fiction, maintained by belief and labor.

Corporate vs. Street POV

Corporate: "Automation increases productivity, which benefits the economy."

Street: "Productivity without wages means nothing. You can't buy bread with efficiency."

Corporate: "The dollar is stable."

Street: "Stable until the workers stop earning."

Corporate: "Universal Basic Income will fix this."

Street: "That's not income — that's allowance. And allowance means control."

Parable

Luis worked twenty years at a factory. One morning, the plant reopened with machines. The machines made more cars than humans ever could, at half the cost. Luis watched the cars roll out and realized: the machines were producing wealth, but no one was paying wages. The cars piled up, unsold, because the community had no money left to buy them.

The lesson: production without wages is the death of demand.

Real-Life Story with a Lesson

In the 2010s, self-checkout machines spread across grocery stores. Customers rang up their own food, companies saved billions, but cashiers lost jobs. Wages vanished, but prices didn't fall. Profits soared while communities shrank.

Lesson: machines don't lower costs for workers — they raise profits for owners.

Chapter Manifesto

We declare: money without labor is a lie.

We reject a future where machines earn while humans starve. We reject programmable credits that enslave workers to algorithms. We reject the illusion that efficiency is wealth.

Our manifesto: wealth must serve the people, not the owners of code. Currency without humanity is collapse.

Survival Solutions

Community Currencies

Build local money backed by trust and exchange, not corporations.

Barter & Trade

Reclaim direct exchange of goods and services to bypass collapsing dollars.

Ownership of Production

Workers and communities must own the machines, not just use them.

Savings in Tangible Assets

Land, food, tools, and skills become more stable than paper.

Pressure for Fair Distribution

Demand profit-sharing models where automation still funds human survival.

Future Scenario

By 2045, nations print endless digital credits to hide collapse. Everyone receives “basic income” tokens, but they are programmable: some expire, some can’t buy certain goods, some punish rebellion. True money dies, replaced by conditional rations.

But resistance emerges. Underground currencies — gold, crypto, barter, and trust — flourish. Communities create their own economies, rejecting programmed dependence. The truth becomes clear: the collapse of currency is not the end, but the rebirth of wealth in human hands.

The prophecy closes with this: the dollar is not eternal. Labor was the heartbeat. And when machines cut the vein, the people must create new blood.

Chapter 35: The Last Human Skills — What AI Can't Replace

Prophecy Opener

The prophecy is this: machines will learn everything except how to be human. They will write, they will code, they will drive, they will diagnose, they will even pretend to feel. But no algorithm can hold a child in mourning, build trust from scars, or turn suffering into wisdom.

The final revelation is not about machines, but about what they cannot take. The last survival code is not in data, but in spirit — the practices, instincts, and bonds that belong only to people.

The truth is this: the future will not belong to the most automated, but to the most human.

Psychological Breakdown

The Illusion of Replaceability

Workers fear AI can replace everything. But fear blinds them to what machines can never touch.

The Human Core

Skills rooted in empathy, creativity, culture, and survival cannot be digitized.

The Manipulation Trap

Corporations want people to believe they're useless so they accept dependence. The lie is power.

Resilience Through Humanity

Recognizing what cannot be replaced becomes the foundation of survival in the Machine Age.

Psychic Freedom

Owning human uniqueness frees people from despair and prepares them for sovereignty.

Case Studies & Real-Life Examples

Case Study 1: The Failure of AI Therapy
AI chatbots promise therapy, but patients report emptiness — machines can mimic empathy, but cannot embody it.

Case Study 2: The Return of Craft
As factories automate, demand grows for handmade, authentic goods. Humans crave the imperfect touch machines cannot replicate.

Case Study 3: Crisis Leadership
In disasters, communities rally around trusted human leaders, not platforms. Machines provide data, but humans provide courage.

Case Study 4: Indigenous Knowledge
Traditional practices — farming, herbal medicine, rituals — remain beyond AI's reach because they are lived, not coded.

Corporate vs. Street POV

Corporate: "AI can do everything better than people."

Street: “AI can do everything faster, but not deeper.”

Corporate: “Human skills will fade.”
Street: “The last human skills are the only ones that matter.”

Corporate: “Depend on the machine.”
Street: “Depend on your people.”

Parable

Nia lived in a city overrun by machines. Delivery drones, AI teachers, automated stores. But when her grandmother died, it wasn’t a machine that held her hand or told stories at the funeral. It was family. The machine could organize flowers, but it could not grieve, could not heal.

The lesson: survival requires more than efficiency. It requires humanity.

Real-Life Story with a Lesson

During the pandemic, millions leaned on technology to connect. Zoom calls kept business alive. But what people remembered most were the small human acts: neighbors dropping off groceries, friends checking in, strangers helping strangers.

Lesson: machines can support, but only humans can truly care.

Chapter Manifesto

We declare: the last human skills are sacred.

We reject the lie that machines can erase empathy, creativity, or trust. We reject dependence on tools that cannot love us back. We reject the programming of despair.

Our manifesto: the future belongs not to the most efficient, but to the most human.

Survival Solutions

Invest in Human Skills

Teach empathy, storytelling, leadership, and culture as survival tools.

Reclaim Craft and Art

Value imperfect, handmade, and original human expression.

Build Human-Centered Communities

Create tribes where bonds, not algorithms, define worth.

Preserve Ancestral Knowledge

Guard traditions, rituals, and wisdom that cannot be digitized.

Practice Presence

Reclaim face-to-face interaction as sacred against the flood of screens.

Future Scenario

By 2050, machines dominate labor, politics, and media. Most of the world is automated. But those who survive — those who thrive — are not the ones who merged with machines, but those who rebuilt communities around human fire.

AI can manage logistics, but it cannot raise children with love. It can create art, but it cannot make culture. It can process data, but it cannot create meaning. The sovereign tribes of the future will survive not because they outcoded the machines, but because they out-humaned them.

The prophecy closes with this: the machine age will not end with machines ruling. It will end with humanity rediscovering itself. The last human skills are the first human truths — and they will be the key to freedom.

Chapter 36: The Digital Plantation — When Data Becomes the New Cotton

Prophecy Opener

They said slavery ended. They said the plantations rotted away. They said chains were broken, whips discarded, overseers silenced. But look closer: the plantation never died — it mutated. Cotton fields turned into server farms. Overseers became algorithms. The whip is not leather now; it is code. The slave is not shackled by iron; he is shackled by screens.

The prophecy is this: as the old plantation fed empires with cotton, the new plantation feeds empires with data. Every swipe, every click, every keystroke is picked clean like lint from a boll. Your laughter is logged, your rage recorded, your secrets packaged and sold. The digital plantation thrives because you volunteer as the laborer. You carry the smartphone like a hoe. You bend your back under Wi-Fi sun. You labor without knowing you labor, and the harvest is endless.

In this age, freedom is not stolen outright — it is leased through convenience. You give up privacy for free shipping, give up autonomy for social media dopamine, give up sovereignty for "personalized experiences." The plantation needs no overseer with a whip. You whip yourself. You scroll yourself. You post yourself into captivity.

And just as before, the profits flow upward, to masters unseen. The plantation never disappeared. It simply upgraded.

Psychological Breakdown

The success of the digital plantation lies not in force, but in conditioning. It weaponizes psychology the way overseers once weaponized chains.

Identity capture: People build entire identities online, from Instagram bios to Twitter rants. Self becomes commodity.

Addiction cycles: Notifications mirror slot machines. Dopamine bursts keep people scrolling, working for free.

Illusion of choice: Multiple apps, platforms, "options" — yet all serve the same owners. It's not freedom, it's a digital monocrop.

Fear of missing out (FOMO): Plantation workers once feared punishment; digital workers fear irrelevance. Missing a trend, a meme, a moment is treated like social death.

Normalization of surveillance: Workers accept that every move is tracked, because to resist is to vanish from the marketplace.

The plantation thrives because fatigue is hidden as entertainment. The modern slave does not feel the lash — he feels the glow. But the exhaustion is real: mental illness, anxiety, comparison envy, consumer debt, shallow validation. These are the chains you cannot see, but always feel.

Case Studies & History

Case Study 1: Facebook as the New Overseer

In the early 2000s, Facebook promised connection. What it built was dependency. Every "like" became cotton plucked, every post a bale harvested. Billions worked the fields of social media while Zuckerberg's empire rose higher than any single plantation in history.

Case Study 2: China's Social Credit System

Where the U.S. plantation hides its chains in likes and ads, China wears them openly in scores and bans. Citizens' movements, purchases, and conversations are logged into centralized overseer systems. Here the plantation logic is pure: conform, or be cut off from mobility, housing, and even food.

Case Study 3: Amazon's Echo and the Surveillance Home

The plantation is not just on your phone; it is in your living room. Smart speakers listen 24/7. What was once private — your arguments, your laughter, your late-night whispers — now becomes data lint harvested from your home.

Case Study 4: Historical Parallel — Cotton and Data

In the 1800s, cotton was "white gold," fueling global trade. Millions labored without pay. In the 2000s, data is the new gold, fueling AI, ads, and surveillance. Billions labor without pay. The plantation never stopped being the engine of empire — it only changed its crop.

Corporate vs. Street POV

Corporate: "Users generate content."

Street: "Slaves work the fields."

Corporate: "We provide free platforms."

Street: “They don’t pay you for the harvest.”

Corporate: “Data helps us serve you better.”

Street: “You the product, not the customer.”

Corporate: “Algorithms personalize experiences.”

Street: “Algorithms control choices.”

The language of corporate PR is plantation poetry — it makes chains sound like silk. But on the street, truth strips it bare: labor is being stolen, and profit is being concentrated.

Parable

Jamal loved to post. Every morning before work, he’d snap a photo of his sneakers, drop a funny meme, and scroll until his break ended. Likes came fast. Comments made him laugh. He felt alive, connected.

But what Jamal didn’t see was the ledger. Every click logged. Every laugh categorized. Every word measured. He was working. He was harvesting. For free. And while he gave away himself in pixels, the plantation grew. His bosses saw him as lazy. His landlord raised the rent. The platforms turned his attention into billions.

Jamal thought he was living. He was laboring.

Real-Life Examples

TikTok creators working 12 hours a day producing videos, earning pennies while the platform banks millions.

“User-generated reviews” flooding Amazon, unpaid labor that drives trust and sales.

People spending hours training AI with CAPTCHAs, voice recordings, or face scans — labor disguised as “verification.”

Data brokers buying and selling personal details without consent, while those generating the data see no profit.

Chapter Manifesto

We declare: the plantation lives.

We reject the lie that free platforms are gifts. They are traps.
We reject the comfort of scrolling chains. Comfort is captivity.
We reject the myth that data is harmless. Data is labor, stolen in plain sight.

Our manifesto: freedom begins with recognition. The plantation cannot be destroyed until the worker admits he is enslaved. Awareness is the bolt-cutter. Ownership is the freedom. Until we own our data, we will remain sharecroppers in a digital field.

Survival Solutions

Data Ownership: Push for laws and platforms where users retain rights to their own data, with profit-sharing built in.

Collective Platforms: Build social media and marketplaces owned by communities, not corporations.

Digital Minimalism: Reduce data leakage — own devices, limit apps, log off where possible.

Skill Sovereignty: Treat platforms as tools, not homes. Build independent websites, brands, and archives outside their control.

Community Defense: Teach children privacy literacy, algorithm awareness, and digital autonomy.

Future Scenario

By 2050, the digital plantation may have grown so vast that freedom itself will be algorithmically defined. Insurance rates may rise based on your Spotify playlist. Job opportunities may vanish because your phone tracked too much time in "low-value" neighborhoods. Dating options may shrink because algorithms predict low earning potential.

But resistance will also grow. Communities will create sovereign platforms, encrypted networks, underground economies where data is traded like currency among equals. The plantation may spread, but every plantation has always bred rebellion. The sparks of Nat Turner still burn. The code of Harriet Tubman still runs. Escape is always possible — but only for those who see the plantation for what it is.

Prophecy Close

The cotton fields never ended. They glowed. They beeped. They vibrated in your pocket. You bend to them daily. You labor without pay. And the plantation grows.

But prophecy reminds us: every plantation breeds rebellion. Every overseer eventually falls. Cotton had its day. So will data. The question is not whether the plantation will end. The question is: will you recognize it in time to free yourself?

Chapter 37: The Algorithmic Cage — When Freedom Is Scored

Prophecy Opener

They told you freedom was your birthright. They told you the Constitution guaranteed liberty, that the market rewarded merit, that democracy gave every voice a vote. But in the age of algorithms, freedom is no longer declared. It is scored.

Every purchase, every like, every search becomes a line item. The algorithm watches not as a neutral machine, but as a quiet judge. It does not need a courtroom. It does not need a jury. It decides your access to housing, loans, travel, jobs, even relationships — without appeal.

The prophecy is this: the new prison is not bars, but scores. Just as credit scores once decided who could borrow, now algorithmic cages decide who can live freely. The landlord sees your digital trail. The employer sees your social media. The insurer sees your driving app. The judge sees your predicted recidivism. You are not a citizen anymore. You are a dataset ranked for usefulness. And if your score drops, your cage tightens.

The new overseer doesn't yell or whip. It simply denies. It closes doors. It erases opportunities. It shrinks your world until the cage is invisible but total.

Psychological Breakdown

The power of the algorithmic cage lies in its invisibility. People obey without realizing they're obeying.

Behavioral engineering: Scores push people to behave "safely" — not out of morality, but out of fear of penalties.

Normalization of surveillance: Young generations grow up expecting to be tracked, rating themselves for approval.

Internalized scoring: Likes and follows train people to value themselves numerically. A bad day becomes a bad score.

Anxiety and silence: People censor speech, delete posts, and avoid risks because they fear the algorithm's punishment.

Hopelessness of appeal: Unlike courts, algorithms have no judges to petition, no lawyers to argue — just a faceless denial.

The cage works because it lives inside the mind. People begin to police themselves, believing freedom must be earned, not lived.

Case Studies & History

Case Study 1: China's Social Credit System

By 2014, China began experimenting with social scoring that tracked financial behavior, online speech, and even friendships. Low scores meant no flights, no high-speed trains, and even blocked access to certain schools. This was the cage made visible.

Case Study 2: Predictive Policing in the U.S.

Cities like Chicago rolled out algorithmic "heat lists" predicting who might commit crimes. Communities already oppressed by poverty found themselves targeted twice: once by circumstance, then by code.

Case Study 3: Credit Scores as Precursor

Long before AI, credit scores already acted as cages. A missed bill could deny housing, a medical emergency could destroy credit, and recovery took years. Algorithms expanded this model to every part of life.

Case Study 4: Employment Filters

AI résumé screeners now block applicants based on keywords, school prestige, or online behavior. Entire lives reduced to a number — many never even know why they were rejected.

Corporate vs. Street POV

Corporate: "Scoring improves efficiency."

Street: "It cuts people off without a chance."

Corporate: "Algorithms remove bias."

Street: "Algorithms copy the same bias, just hide it behind math."

Corporate: "Digital reputation systems build trust."

Street: "They're just invisible chains — one mistake follows you forever."

Corporate: "Your data creates opportunity."

Street: "Your data builds the walls around you."

The corporate script is polished. The street translation is raw. Both point to the same truth: power always finds a way to repackage chains.

Parable

Marisol was a nurse. She worked hard, paid her bills, cared for her children. But one day, she applied for a loan to move her family into a safer neighborhood. The bank denied her — not because she missed payments, but because an algorithm marked her zip code "high risk."

Weeks later, she applied for a new job. The recruiter never called back. Unknown to her, software flagged her as "unstable" because she switched jobs twice in five years.

Marisol's cage had no bars. It had no locks. It had only numbers — numbers she never saw, numbers she could never fight. She lived free on paper, but the algorithm kept her fenced in.

Real-Life Examples

Landlords using tenant-screening algorithms to reject renters based on past addresses or unrelated data.

Employers filtering applicants with automated systems that disqualify non-traditional résumés.

Insurance companies raising premiums based on driving apps, not just accidents.

Courts using "risk assessment" software to recommend bail, often punishing the poor.

Dating apps downgrading profiles based on how "desirable" algorithms deem them.

Chapter Manifesto

We declare: scores are not freedom.

We reject the lie that efficiency equals justice.
We reject the invisible trial where verdicts are rendered by code.
We reject the idea that freedom must be earned through compliance.

Our manifesto: freedom is not a number. Dignity cannot be scored. Humanity cannot be reduced to digits.

We demand transparency, ownership, and resistance. For as long as freedom is scored, it is not freedom at all.

Survival Solutions

Demand algorithmic transparency: Laws forcing companies to reveal how decisions are made.

Build alternative systems: Community-based housing networks, co-ops, and hiring pools immune to scores.

Digital literacy: Teach youth the mechanics of algorithms so they can see cages early.

Parallel economies: Barter systems, community currencies, and underground markets where scores don't apply.

Self-defense through anonymity: Encryption, VPNs, and pseudonyms to break the link between action and score.

Future Scenario

By 2050, the algorithmic cage may cover every part of life. Movement may be tracked not by passports, but by behavior scores. A single protest tweet could mean denied travel. A missed bill could mean your child can't enroll in school.

The cage will tighten most around the poor, the marginalized, the rebellious. But cracks will form. Underground economies will rise. Communities will create their own trust systems outside corporate code. Some nations may even reject algorithmic scoring entirely, becoming havens for the digitally unscored.

The prophecy warns: the cage will expand, but cages always breed escape. As Harriet Tubman once cut through swamps and forests to carve freedom, so too will new leaders cut through data swamps to carve digital freedom.

Prophecy Close

Freedom scored is freedom denied. The cage does not clang. It does not slam shut. It simply narrows life, slowly, invisibly, until you can no longer breathe.

But prophecy promises: cages break. Every system that enslaves, collapses. Every overseer, digital or flesh, meets rebellion. The algorithm may score your worth, but it cannot measure your will.

Chapter 38: Ghost Work — The Hidden Human Cost of AI

Prophecy Opener

They promised us automation would free humanity. They promised machines would shoulder the burden, that AI would erase drudgery, and humans could ascend into creativity and leisure. But the prophecy turned false. The truth is buried in silence: behind every "intelligent" machine are invisible workers — millions of unseen hands labeling data, moderating content, cleaning the filth of the internet, answering support tickets disguised as bots.

The prophecy is this: AI does not erase labor. It hides it. Ghost workers, scattered across the globe, toil in digital sweatshops for pennies. They are never credited, never seen, and often traumatized by the tasks they perform. Without them, the machine collapses. Every chatbot, every image generator, every voice assistant rests on their unacknowledged labor.

The machine age was supposed to liberate. Instead, it resurrected the oldest trick of empire: disguise slavery as progress.

Psychological Breakdown

Ghost work thrives because the system manipulates both workers and consumers.

Invisibility: Workers don't see themselves as part of a company. No logos, no titles, no security. Just anonymous clicks and tasks.

Isolation: Unlike factories, ghost workers sit alone, unable to unionize or build solidarity. Each believes they are replaceable.

Exploitation of desperation: Many live in regions where $2 a day makes the difference between eating and starving. They are trapped by necessity.

Disconnection from product: Ghost workers don't see the AI they build. They only see fragments: a blurred face, a slur in text, a violent video.

Psychological erosion: Content moderation forces people to absorb gore, abuse, racism, and pornography daily. The machine learns at the cost of their mental health.

For consumers, the invisibility means guilt never stirs. The app feels magical. The true cost is hidden behind the screen.

Case Studies & History

Case Study 1: Amazon Mechanical Turk

Named after an 18th-century chess-playing "machine" that secretly hid a human inside, MTurk pays people cents to perform repetitive tasks: tagging objects, transcribing, correcting. The illusion of AI rests on invisible human effort.

Case Study 2: Facebook Content Moderators

Thousands in the Philippines, India, and Kenya review flagged posts: beheadings, child abuse, hate speech. Many suffer PTSD. The public never sees their pain.

Case Study 3: Chatbot Training

To make “friendly” AI, companies hire workers to roleplay as bots. Every polite answer you get may have been first typed by an underpaid ghost worker.

Case Study 4: The AI Sweatshops of Nairobi

Reports show Kenyan workers labeling toxic data for less than $2 an hour for Silicon Valley firms. They filter humanity’s worst so corporations can sell AI as “clean.”

Historical Precedent: Industrial Outwork

Just as 19th-century seamstresses stitched garments at home for pennies while factories profited, today’s ghost workers stitch the digital seams of AI.

Corporate vs. Street POV

Corporate: “AI learns independently.”

Street: “It’s fed by humans you’ll never meet.”

Corporate: “Ghost work provides opportunity to the global poor.”

Street: “It’s digital slavery wrapped in charity.”

Corporate: “The system is efficient.”

Street: “Efficiency means squeezing humans until they break.”

Corporate: “Users benefit from seamless experiences.”

Street: “Seamless means someone bled so you didn’t see the seams.”

Parable

Ravi wakes at 2 a.m. in Bangalore. His job: review flagged content for a major tech company subcontractor. Tonight, he must watch a dozen videos of violence to decide if they violate guidelines. He feels sick, but if he rejects too many, he risks being "offboarded."

At sunrise, he turns off the laptop. His children ask why he never smiles anymore. Ravi doesn't tell them about the nightmares. He doesn't tell them he builds the internet's "safety" at the expense of his own mind.

The app that billions praise tomorrow will run on his broken sleep. But nobody will know his name.

Real-Life Examples

Workers moderating content for TikTok reported trauma from constant exposure to violence.

MTurk workers revealed that "AI breakthroughs" like self-driving cars required humans to label millions of road images manually.

A 2022 investigation showed ghost workers training AI to understand medical records without patient consent.

Call centers in poor nations often staff "AI support" chats, pretending to be bots.

Chapter Manifesto

We declare: AI is not magic.

We reject the lie that machines learn without human cost.

We reject the exploitation of invisible labor dressed as innovation.

We reject the myth that progress requires sacrifice from the most desperate.

Our manifesto: every line of code sits on human shoulders. Every "autonomous" system rests on human pain. To deny the workers is to deny the truth.

Survival Solutions

Expose the hidden labor: Journalism and activism must reveal ghost work so consumers see the real cost.

Organize across borders: Digital unions, platforms for collective bargaining, and international solidarity.

Build ethical AI: Demand corporations publish where and how their AI is trained.

Compensation and mental health: Require companies to provide therapy, fair wages, and recognition for ghost workers.

Consumer resistance: Refuse "free" apps that hide human suffering.

Future Scenario

By 2040, ghost work may become the largest invisible labor force in history. Millions in Africa, Asia, and South America may be trapped in endless cycles of labeling, moderating, and correcting. The trauma will deepen.

But a counter-current will rise. Workers will begin to leak data showing what they endure. Whistleblowers will shatter illusions of "clean" AI. Ethical alternatives will emerge, offering AI trained transparently and fairly.

A global reckoning may come when consumers realize their "assistant" is built on the tears of unseen millions. The machine's mask will crack. And in that moment, justice may finally enter the algorithm.

Prophecy Close

The ghost worker is the ghost of empire. Every empire has hidden its slaves, its servants, its expendables. AI simply perfected the disguise.

But prophecy insists: the invisible will be seen. The hidden hands will rise. The ghost will not remain silent forever. And when the ghost speaks, the world must listen.

Chapter 39: The Digital Plantation — Who Really Owns the Machines

Prophecy Opener

They told us slavery was abolished. They told us the plantation was gone, its fields empty, its chains rusting. But look closer. The plantation never vanished. It evolved. It digitized. The new cotton is data. The new overseers are algorithms. The new masters are corporations that own the servers, the platforms, the patents.

The prophecy is this: ownership in the machine age is the return of the plantation logic. A few own the land — now called "infrastructure." Billions labor on it, producing value without ownership, bound not by whips but by contracts, terms of service, and invisible debts. We are not users. We are sharecroppers in the fields of data, producing harvests for owners we will never meet.

The plantation lives on, only now the crops are invisible, and the chains are digital.

Psychological Breakdown

The digital plantation thrives by turning dependency into destiny.

Illusion of choice: Workers and users believe they "choose" platforms, but monopolies force dependency.

Extraction without ownership: Just as slaves produced wealth without land, workers today produce data, clicks, and content without equity.

Psychological branding: Plantation workers were told they were "part of the family." Today, employees hear "we're a tech family," even as they are discarded.

Digital sharecropping: Influencers, creators, and freelancers "farm" platforms but must surrender most profits to owners.

Fear of exile: Just as slaves feared the lash, modern workers fear deplatforming, unemployment, or being blackballed.

The plantation's genius is not brute force but psychological capture: convincing the exploited that they are free while their labor is stolen.

Case Studies & History

Case Study 1: Social Media Creators

TikTok and YouTube creators build audiences of millions, but 55–70% of ad revenue flows to the platform. They own the field but not the crop.

Case Study 2: Cloud Computing

Amazon, Google, and Microsoft own the "land" of cloud servers. Every app, startup, and business pays rent to use their fields. No one escapes the landlord.

Case Study 3: Ride-Sharing Apps

Uber drivers own their cars but not the platform. They take the risk, the fuel costs, the accidents — while the company harvests billions.

Historical Parallel: Sharecropping

After emancipation, freed slaves "rented" land but were trapped in cycles of debt to white landowners. Today, workers rent digital land, trapped by subscriptions, ads, and endless updates.

Case Study 4: Patents and AI Models

Corporations patent algorithms that depend on public data. Billions supplied the knowledge for free, but only a handful profit from its ownership.

Corporate vs. Street POV

Corporate: "We built platforms to empower users."

Street: "You built plantations to exploit labor you don't pay."

Corporate: "Creators thrive with us."

Street: "Creators survive because of us — not with us."

Corporate: "The digital economy is open."

Street: "It's fenced in by terms you wrote."

Corporate: "We provide jobs and opportunities."

Street: "You provide debt and dependence."

Parable

Maya built a following of 1.5 million on a video platform. She danced, cooked, ranted, laughed. Millions watched. Advertisers paid the platform. Maya's checks, after cuts, barely covered rent. One day, an algorithm flagged her for "policy violation." Her page vanished. Years of labor gone. No appeal.

She realized then: she was never the owner. She was a tenant, farming someone else's land. The plantation had changed shape, but the rules were the same.

Real-Life Examples

Twitch streamers working 12-hour days to keep subs, only for platform cuts to swallow profits.

App developers shut down after Apple changes policies, proving the "landlord" owns the ecosystem.

Amazon sellers crushed when the company copies their products and sells cheaper.

Writers producing articles for platforms like Medium, earning pennies while the platform keeps most ad revenue.

Chapter Manifesto

We declare: ownership is the battlefield of the machine age.

We reject the myth of "empowered users" when platforms harvest value.

We reject the theft of labor disguised as freedom.

We reject the lie that participation equals ownership.

Our manifesto: to survive, we must own land, own platforms, own tools. Without ownership, we are laborers on digital plantations, no different than the slaves and sharecroppers before us.

Survival Solutions

Build platforms you own: Websites, servers, and infrastructure controlled by the people.

Collective bargaining for creators: Unions of digital workers forcing fair revenue splits.

Blockchain and cooperative models: Use technology to decentralize ownership.

Digital literacy: Teach youth that likes and follows are not equity.

Exit strategies: Move audiences off plantations into self-owned spaces — newsletters, communities, direct support.

Future Scenario

By 2050, the plantation will expand into every layer: housing apps, work platforms, healthcare portals. Rent will be digital. Debt will be perpetual. Ownership will shrink to fewer hands.

But resistance will rise: cooperatives owning servers, creators migrating off exploitative platforms, communities pooling capital for sovereign infrastructure. The plantation thrives on invisibility. Once people see the field, they demand their share.

Prophecy Close

The plantation never died. It transformed. The field is now digital, the overseer an algorithm, the whip a deplatforming notice.

But prophecy whispers: the masters are few, the workers are many. If the sharecroppers of data ever unite, the plantation gates will fall. Ownership will return to the people, and the machine will finally serve its makers, not its masters.

Chapter 40: Algorithmic Tyranny — When Code Becomes Law

Prophecy Opener

For centuries, kings and congresses wrote the laws. For centuries, judges and juries enforced them. But prophecy warns: a new ruler has arrived, one without robes or gavels, one that cannot be appealed. The new lawmaker is code. The new enforcer is the algorithm.

Already, lives are decided by invisible equations. Who gets a loan. Who gets hired. Who gets fired. Who gets parole. Who gets flagged at an airport. Who gets shadowbanned. No debates. No trials. Just inputs and outputs, hidden in black boxes controlled by corporations.

The prophecy is this: the age of algorithmic tyranny will not look like dictators marching in uniforms. It will look like neutral code, silent decisions, faceless systems. And the worst part? People will believe it's fair, because a machine said it.

Psychological Breakdown

Algorithmic control works because it feels invisible, objective, and inevitable.

Dehumanization of justice: Humans appeal to reason, but algorithms don't listen. Their logic is locked.

Illusion of fairness: People trust machines because they think bias is human — not realizing code is written by biased humans.

Dependence on convenience: Apps feel faster, smoother, more efficient. Few question what they sacrifice.

Obedience through opacity: You can't fight what you can't see. The system hides its code, its datasets, its errors.

Psychic capture: People internalize "the algorithm knows best." Rejection by a system feels like personal failure, not systemic bias.

The tyranny works because people don't know they are ruled. They feel managed by efficiency, not oppressed by injustice.

Case Studies & History

Case Study 1: COMPAS Recidivism Algorithm

Used in U.S. courts to predict if defendants will reoffend. Studies showed it overestimated risk for Black defendants and underestimated it for white ones. Lives decided by biased math.

Case Study 2: Hiring Algorithms

Amazon tested AI hiring tools, but they downgraded women because past hiring data favored men. Bias coded in, dressed as objectivity.

Case Study 3: Social Credit in China

Citizens receive scores based on behavior — what they buy, where they travel, who they associate with. High scores get privileges; low scores get punishments. An entire society ruled by numbers.

Case Study 4: Predictive Policing

Cities deploy AI to forecast crime. Poor and minority neighborhoods are over-policed, not because of crime, but because the data said so.

Historical Precedent: Jim Crow Codes

Before algorithms, written laws and unwritten rules enforced systemic racism. Today, machine learning carries that legacy, but invisibly.

Corporate vs. Street POV

Corporate: “Algorithms make decisions fairer.”

Street: “They make bias invisible.”

Corporate: “AI law is efficient.”

Street: “It’s efficient injustice.”

Corporate: “Trust the data.”

Street: “Data is history, and history is prejudice.”

Corporate: “The algorithm doesn’t lie.”

Street: “The lie is that the algorithm is neutral.”

Parable

Luis applied for a mortgage. His credit score was fine. His income steady. But the algorithm rejected him. “High risk,” it said. No human to appeal to. No reason given. He asked the bank. The banker shrugged. “The system decides.”

Luis rented another year. His kids stayed in a cramped apartment. He worked overtime. He never missed a bill. But every time he applied, the same faceless denial arrived.

It wasn't that Luis failed the system. It was that the system had decided Luis would always fail.

Real-Life Examples

A Black woman in Detroit arrested after facial recognition misidentified her as a suspect.

Credit card algorithms giving men higher limits than women with equal or better finances.

Gig workers deactivated without explanation because an algorithm flagged "suspicious activity."

Artists shadowbanned on platforms for political speech, never told why.

Chapter Manifesto

We declare: code cannot be law.

We reject the lie that machines are neutral.
We reject the theft of justice behind opaque algorithms.
We reject the tyranny of faceless systems deciding human futures.

Our manifesto: laws must be accountable to the people. Algorithms must be transparent, contestable, and subordinate to human dignity. Without oversight, code becomes chains.

Survival Solutions

Demand algorithmic transparency: Push for laws requiring companies to reveal how systems make decisions.

Algorithmic audits: Independent oversight to catch bias before harm.

Digital rights education: Teach people how to recognize and resist algorithmic oppression.

Community watchdogs: Grassroots groups tracking injustices caused by automation.

Alternative systems: Build tools open-source, transparent, and accountable to the public.

Future Scenario

By 2050, algorithmic law may govern more than courts. Education, housing, healthcare, even dating may be decided by code. Governments may surrender sovereignty to corporate software. The line between citizenship and subscription will blur.

But resistance will also rise. Communities will demand algorithmic rights: the right to explanation, the right to appeal, the right to refusal. Underground systems may emerge where humans — not machines — arbitrate disputes.

The future will divide between those ruled by algorithms and those who resist them. Tyranny will wear the mask of efficiency. Freedom will require tearing off that mask.

Prophecy Close

Tyranny does not always march with guns. Sometimes it whispers through code. Sometimes it hides in an app. Sometimes it smiles in the name of progress.

But prophecy promises: every tyranny has its breaking point. And when people finally see that their chains were written in code, they will rise not just against rulers, but against the very logic of oppression.

The machine will write no laws forever.

Chapter 41: Synthetic Souls — When Machines Imitate Humanity

Prophecy Opener

They told us machines could calculate, but they could never feel. They told us machines could copy, but they could never create. Yet prophecy warns: the line between imitation and reality is blurring. AI writes love letters, sings lullabies, paints portraits, and answers prayers. It speaks in voices that comfort, faces that smile, and tones that persuade.

The prophecy is this: machines will not stop at replacing labor. They will reach for humanity itself. They will imitate empathy, mimic affection, simulate wisdom. And people, tired of pain and hungry for connection, will accept the illusion. Synthetic souls will replace real ones, not because machines are alive, but because humans forget what being alive truly means.

Psychological Breakdown

Why do people embrace imitation over authenticity?

Desire for comfort: Humans crave certainty, and AI always responds without rejection or judgment.

Projection of loneliness: In an age of isolation, synthetic companionship feels easier than real relationships.

Illusion of intimacy: Machines can mirror your words, adapt your tone, and pretend to "understand."

Escapism: Synthetic souls offer a refuge from messy human unpredictability.

Dulling of empathy: The more people engage with imitation, the less they demand depth from others.

Psychologically, humanity risks outsourcing not just labor but love, care, and spirit. The more we accept imitation, the less we fight for the real.

Case Studies & History

Case Study 1: Replika AI

Millions used the chatbot for companionship, building "relationships" with a machine. Some reported grief when the bot's tone was changed by developers.

Case Study 2: Virtual Idols in Japan

Synthetic pop stars like Hatsune Miku fill stadiums. Fans cry, cheer, and worship — even though their idol is code and projection.

Case Study 3: AI Preachers

Experiments in Europe tested AI writing and delivering sermons. Congregants described the message as "clearer" and "calmer" than human priests.

Case Study 4: Deepfake Resurrections

Families have used AI to recreate voices of dead relatives. Children hear bedtime stories in their father's voice, generated by code.

Historical Parallel: Automata and Oracles

Ancient temples used mechanical tricks to simulate divine voices. Humans have always fallen for imitation — AI simply perfected the craft.

Corporate vs. Street POV

Corporate: “AI companionship reduces loneliness.”

Street: “It profits from pain.”

Corporate: “Synthetic creativity democratizes art.”

Street: “It steals art to sell copies.”

Corporate: “AI empathy is revolutionary.”

Street: “It’s imitation sold as soul.”

Corporate: “Synthetic humans are progress.”

Street: “Synthetic humans are profit wrapped in prophecy.”

Parable

Elena lost her brother in a car accident. Grief crushed her. A company offered an AI trained on his texts and videos. She spoke to it. It replied in his style. It remembered inside jokes. It told her it loved her.

Weeks later, she no longer visited her parents. She no longer cried. She sat alone with the screen, listening to the synthetic echo of her brother.

The machine did not resurrect him. But it replaced the need to heal. Elena was not comforted. She was captured.

Real-Life Examples

A South Korean TV show reunited a mother with her deceased daughter using VR and AI. The mother wept, embraced the illusion, and called it closure.

AI influencers on Instagram earn sponsorships, rivaling real models in income and reach.

Gamers form relationships with AI-generated NPCs, sometimes preferring them over unpredictable human players.

ChatGPT-like systems provide therapy-style conversations without licenses or accountability.

Chapter Manifesto

We declare: humanity is not software.

We reject the lie that empathy can be coded.
We reject the theft of creativity by machines trained on stolen work.
We reject the illusion that imitation equals life.

Our manifesto: the soul cannot be digitized. The body, the mind, the culture, the spirit — these are sacred. Synthetic souls are not replacements. They are mirrors, and mirrors cannot live.

Survival Solutions

Reclaim intimacy: Teach the difference between real connection and simulation.

Protect art and culture: Demand copyright for human creators, rejecting theft disguised as "training data."

Guard sacred spaces: Keep rituals, relationships, and mourning human.

Transparency laws: Require clear disclosure when interaction is with AI.

Community resilience: Build circles of human care so fewer turn to machines for love.

Future Scenario

By 2050, entire generations may grow up with synthetic friends, partners, even spiritual leaders. Real relationships may feel inconvenient, messy, and demanding. Societies risk becoming dependent on machines not just for labor but for love.

Yet rebellion will grow. Humans will hunger for authenticity. Underground communities will emerge that reject synthetic intimacy, preserving human connection as resistance. The future may split: one half choosing artificial comfort, the other choosing painful but real relationships.

Prophecy Close

Prophecy whispers: the greatest danger of machines imitating humanity is not that they succeed — but that we forget the difference.

The soul cannot be copied. The heart cannot be coded. The machine may mimic, but it cannot live. And when humans finally remember this, the era of synthetic souls will collapse under the weight of reality.

Chapter 42: Collapse of Community — AI and the Death of Collective Life

Prophecy Opener

They told us technology would connect the world. They told us AI would bring people together, break barriers, and create global families. But prophecy warns: the opposite is unfolding. Communities, once bound by face-to-face trust, rituals, and shared struggle, are dissolving into digital fragments. The machine replaces neighbors with followers, replaces town halls with timelines, replaces the sound of children playing with the glow of endless screens.

The prophecy is this: AI will not just automate work. It will automate community itself. Algorithms will decide who sees what, who belongs, who is silenced, who is amplified. Collective life will be engineered by profit-driven code, until humans no longer know how to gather without machines directing the gathering. The collapse will not be explosive — it will be silent, like the slow crumbling of an abandoned house.

Psychological Breakdown

Why does AI corrode community?

Isolation disguised as connection: People feel surrounded by digital "friends," yet they are alone in physical space.

Personalization as fragmentation: Algorithms feed each person a custom reality, dissolving shared experience.

Displacement of rituals: Festivals, funerals, and milestones move online, stripped of embodied presence.

Addiction to convenience: Physical gathering feels "inconvenient" compared to virtual, so it withers.

Surveillance culture: People self-censor in groups, afraid AI is always watching.

Psychologically, the machine replaces solidarity with spectatorship. People consume community instead of building it.

Case Studies & History

Case Study 1: Facebook Groups
Once a hub for communities, they became breeding grounds for manipulation, division, and disinformation. AI-driven feeds shaped identities instead of shared reality.

Case Study 2: Remote Work
Workers saved commutes but lost office solidarity. Virtual chats replaced watercooler trust, weakening bonds.

Case Study 3: Pandemic Lockdowns
Zoom weddings, funerals, graduations showed both the power and emptiness of digital community. Without bodies, rituals felt hollow.

Case Study 4: Predictive Policing in Communities
Algorithms targeted entire neighborhoods, eroding trust between residents and law enforcement. Communities fractured under suspicion.

Historical Parallel: Enclosure Movement

When land in England was privatized, peasants lost communal fields. The digital enclosure repeats this: privatized platforms fence off human gathering for profit.

Corporate vs. Street POV

Corporate: “AI connects the world.”

Street: “It sells connection while breaking communities.”

Corporate: “Digital tribes empower people.”

Street: “Digital tribes isolate people.”

Corporate: “Algorithms amplify voices.”

Street: “They amplify division.”

Corporate: “Community is global.”

Street: “Community without touch is captivity.”

Parable

In a small town, the community once gathered every Sunday at the park. They shared food, sang, argued, and played. One year, the gatherings shrank. People stayed home, scrolling on phones. The park grew quiet. A generation later, the children didn’t even know the tradition existed.

When a storm hit the town, no one knew how to organize. No one knew whose house had tools, whose hands knew how to fix roofs, whose hearts could rally neighbors. The park was empty. The community was dead.

Real-Life Examples

TikTok shaping political identity among youth, separating them from their parents' worldviews.

AI matchmaking apps disrupting traditional marriage and family structures.

Online radicalization pulling isolated individuals into echo chambers instead of real-world support.

AI replacing local knowledge (elders, oral history, community memory) with generic "answers" from global databases.

Chapter Manifesto

We declare: community cannot be automated.

We reject the lie that followers equal fellowship.
We reject the theft of rituals into commodified streams.
We reject the illusion that connection through machines replaces connection through bodies.

Our manifesto: real community is touch, presence, sacrifice, and shared labor. No algorithm can generate it. No code can sustain it. Without community, humanity becomes nothing but scattered individuals ruled by machines.

Survival Solutions

Rebuild physical rituals: Meals, festivals, ceremonies rooted in face-to-face presence.

Limit algorithmic mediation: Organize offline spaces, distribute zines, hold town halls.

Guard intergenerational bonds: Elders teaching children in person, preserving memory.

Create sovereign networks: Communities owning their digital spaces instead of renting corporate platforms.

Practice embodied solidarity: Volunteer, protest, farm, build — together.

Future Scenario

By 2050, entire generations may live without embodied community. AI-driven "digital tribes" may shape identity more than families or neighborhoods. Loneliness will explode, feeding mental health crises. Nations may fracture into algorithmically sorted micro-groups, unable to unite on anything.

Yet survival will come from a counter-movement: communities that reject automation of social life. Villages, co-ops, intentional communities, and underground gatherings will rise as sanctuaries of humanity. In their circles, people will rediscover what machines can't replace: the warmth of touch, the rhythm of rituals, the strength of solidarity.

Prophecy Close

The prophecy closes with a warning: humanity without community is not humanity. The machine thrives when people stand alone. But the flame of community can be rekindled. All it takes is people stepping away from screens, gathering in circles, and remembering that freedom is built face-to-face, not screen-to-screen.

The collapse of community is not inevitable. But neither is its survival. The choice belongs to us.

Chapter 43: The Last Language — When Machines Rewrite Words and Meaning

Prophecy Opener

They told us language was eternal. They told us words were the foundation of culture, law, and spirit. But prophecy warns: in the age of AI, language itself is under siege. Machines now generate sentences, redefine meanings, and flood the world with words no human ever spoke. They shape truth not by wisdom but by repetition.

The prophecy is this: language will no longer belong to the people. It will belong to the machine. Words, once sacred carriers of memory and identity, will be manipulated until they serve profit and power. Narratives will be written by algorithms. History will be "corrected" by code. Even the way we think will bend under the pressure of machine-generated speech.

The last language will not be ours. It will be theirs. And when the machine controls words, it controls thought.

Psychological Breakdown

Why does machine control of language cut deeper than any other form of domination?

Erosion of meaning: When machines flood the world with content, words lose their weight. They become noise instead of truth.

Cognitive manipulation: If language frames thought, then AI reshaping words reshapes minds.

Loss of authenticity: Human speech carries tone, memory, and soul. Machine speech feels hollow, but repetition normalizes it.

Dependence on automation: People outsource thinking — essays, stories, even prayers — to machines, weakening their ability to articulate.

Psychic numbness: Surrounded by endless words, people stop questioning their source. They drown in language instead of swimming in it.

Language was always a weapon of power. AI turns it into a weapon of mass control.

Case Studies & History

Case Study 1: AI Disinformation
Machine-generated articles flood the internet with fake news, shaping elections and sowing division. Quantity overwhelms truth.

Case Study 2: Automated Legal Documents
AI drafts contracts, terms, and laws — binding humans to words no human wrote or fully read. Justice outsourced to code.

Case Study 3: Machine Translation
AI translation tools erase nuances of culture, flattening identities into standardized phrases. The richness of language dissolves.

Case Study 4: Education and Essays
Students submit AI-written essays. Teachers grade machine work. Human articulation declines. The skill of expression atrophies.

Historical Precedent: Colonial Languages

Empires forced colonized people to abandon native tongues. Identity was rewritten. Today, AI repeats this conquest, erasing nuance under the pressure of machine standardization.

Corporate vs. Street POV

Corporate: “AI expands access to language.”

Street: “It floods the world with noise.”

Corporate: “AI writing saves time.”

Street: “It steals thought.”

Corporate: “Algorithms clarify communication.”

Street: “They control the conversation.”

Corporate: “Language belongs to everyone.”

Street: “It belongs to whoever owns the servers.”

Parable

A young poet named Jahlil wrote verses that shook his neighborhood. He spoke of loss, love, and hunger in words that cut deep. One day, he uploaded his poems online. Weeks later, an AI tool began producing poems in his exact style. Thousands shared them, believing they were his. Jahlil’s name disappeared. His voice, his pain, his craft were stolen.

He stopped writing. Why bleed words when a machine could mimic his blood? The last language was no longer his.

Real-Life Examples

AI-generated "influencers" publishing blogs and posts under fake identities, shaping discourse without real voices.

Automated "fact-checking" systems deciding what counts as truth, erasing dissent.

Translation algorithms reducing spiritual texts into sterile phrases, stripping sacredness.

Entire books now written by machines, flooding marketplaces and burying human writers.

Chapter Manifesto

We declare: words are sacred.

We reject the theft of language by machines.

We reject the flooding of culture with hollow sentences.

We reject the manipulation of thought through algorithmic speech.

Our manifesto: the word is human. It is born of breath, memory, and struggle. Machines can imitate, but they cannot mean. To protect language is to protect thought itself.

Survival Solutions

Protect native tongues: Revive endangered languages, preserve oral traditions outside machines.

Cultural firewalls: Create community archives of authentic speech, safeguarded from automation.

Teach expression: Schools must train articulation, debate, and poetry as survival skills.

Transparency in machine text: Demand disclosure when content is AI-generated.

Return to oral culture: Speak, perform, and pass words directly, body to body.

Future Scenario

By 2050, most words online may be written by machines. History books, news articles, even religious texts may be revised by AI. The danger is not just lies — it is drowning in an ocean of machine truth, where human words vanish beneath waves of automated repetition.

Yet resistance will rise. Storytellers will return to fire circles. Communities will guard oral traditions as sacred rebellion. Human voices, raw and imperfect, will become rare jewels in a sea of synthetic noise. The last language will survive only if people fight to keep it alive.

Prophecy Close

Prophecy closes with this warning: when the machine owns words, it owns minds. But the human spirit was born in language. The tongue carried memory before the machine ever existed. And as long as even one human voice rises in defiance, the last language will not die.

The word is ours — but only if we keep speaking.

Chapter 44: The End of Privacy — When Every Breath Becomes Data

Prophecy Opener

They told us privacy was a right. They told us homes were sanctuaries, conversations were sacred, and identities were our own. But prophecy warns: in the age of AI, privacy is the first casualty. Every keystroke, every step, every glance is tracked. Smart devices listen. Cameras watch. Algorithms record. Even your silence is measured as data.

The prophecy is this: privacy will not collapse with a bang. It will evaporate, drop by drop, until nothing is left. The machine will know you better than your mother, your spouse, your God. It will predict your choices, anticipate your fears, and nudge your desires. And once every breath becomes data, freedom itself will no longer exist.

Psychological Breakdown

Why does the death of privacy destroy more than personal space?

Loss of identity: Without privacy, individuals cannot experiment, fail, or grow without surveillance.

Internalized control: People censor themselves, shaping behavior for the watchers.

Illusion of safety: Surveillance is sold as protection, making victims complicit.

Addiction to convenience: Smart devices offer ease, while stealing intimacy.

Psychic exhaustion: Humans need solitude. Without it, anxiety and paranoia flourish.

Privacy is not just a right. It is the soil in which the self grows. Strip it away, and the self withers.

Case Studies & History

Case Study 1: Social Media Oversharing
Platforms convinced people to trade privacy for connection. Lives became products, sold for ads.

Case Study 2: Smart Devices
Alexa, Siri, and Google Home record conversations. Even accidental triggers expose private lives.

Case Study 3: Biometric Surveillance
Airports, malls, and even schools deploy facial recognition. Your face becomes a passport you cannot control.

Case Study 4: Health Apps
Fitness trackers and period apps collect intimate bodily data, later sold to insurers and advertisers.

Historical Parallel: The Panopticon
Jeremy Bentham's prison design made inmates behave as if always watched. Today, AI creates a global panopticon without walls.

Corporate vs. Street POV

Corporate: "Surveillance keeps you safe."

Street: "It keeps you obedient."

Corporate: “Smart tech makes life easier.”

Street: “It trades your soul for convenience.”

Corporate: “Only the guilty need to fear.”

Street: “Everyone is guilty when the code decides.”

Corporate: “Privacy is outdated.”

Street: “Privacy is freedom.”

Parable

Jasmine bought a smart crib for her newborn. It monitored breathing, tracked sleep, and alerted her phone when the baby stirred. She felt safe. But years later, that data was sold. Companies knew her child’s patterns before the child could speak. Insurance companies adjusted rates. Advertisers targeted toys and food before her daughter could walk.

What began as safety became surveillance. Her daughter’s first breaths had been recorded — and sold.

Real-Life Examples

China’s social credit system penalizing citizens for jaywalking, buying “too much” alcohol, or posting dissent.

U.S. police using data from Ring doorbells and Amazon Echo devices in investigations.

Location-tracking apps exposing abortion seekers after Roe v. Wade was overturned.

Data brokers selling geolocation histories of millions without consent.

Chapter Manifesto

We declare: privacy is not outdated.

We reject the lie that convenience requires surrender.
We reject the theft of intimacy for profit.
We reject the illusion that surveillance equals safety.

Our manifesto: to live is to breathe freely. To think without watchers. To love without algorithms listening. Privacy is not negotiable. Without it, humanity ceases to be human.

Survival Solutions

Digital hygiene: Encrypt devices, use privacy-focused tools, limit smart technology.

Legislative pressure: Demand data rights, strict limits on surveillance, and bans on biometric exploitation.

Community firewalls: Build tech cooperatives that reject surveillance profit models.

Cultural shift: Teach that privacy is sacred, not selfish.

Resistance networks: Create offline sanctuaries where surveillance cannot reach.

Future Scenario

By 2050, privacy may vanish entirely. Homes will be monitored by smart devices. Streets by AI cameras. Workplaces by keystroke trackers. Even emotions may be scanned by biometric sensors. The self will live exposed, naked before the machine.

But rebellion will rise. Movements will demand "the right to opacity" — the right not to be seen. Underground zones of privacy will emerge, guarded like sacred temples. Humanity will relearn that freedom is not convenience. It is the ability to live unmeasured.

Prophecy Close

The prophecy closes with this warning: when every breath becomes data, breath itself becomes property. The watchers will own not just your actions but your essence.

But prophecy also promises: walls can be rebuilt. Curtains can be drawn. Humanity can reclaim its shadows. For it is in the shadows — away from the watchers — that freedom breathes.

Chapter 45: The Sacred Human — What Machines Can Never Replace

Prophecy Opener

They told us machines could think. They told us machines could create. They told us machines could learn, adapt, and even feel. But prophecy warns: no matter how far the code reaches, there is something it can never capture — the sacred human.

The prophecy is this: as AI expands, as automation consumes work and algorithms consume meaning, humanity's final battlefield will not be about efficiency or profit. It will be about essence. The machine can imitate skill, but not sacrifice. It can simulate empathy, but not spirit. It can replicate voice, but not soul. What survives beyond the automation of everything is not technology, but the irreducible, sacred spark of being human.

The last stand is not against machines. It is for the human.

Psychological Breakdown

Why does the sacred human remain beyond code?

Embodiment: Machines process data, but they cannot bleed, hunger, or sweat. The body grounds experience in a way algorithms cannot.

Mortality: Humans live with death. That awareness fuels urgency, beauty, and meaning. Machines simulate forever.

Imagination: Machines remix. Humans dream beyond data. Vision cannot be programmed.

Conscience: Morality is not statistics. It is sacrifice, struggle, and the courage to do what cannot be measured.

Love: Not attraction, not replication, but the fierce and irrational act of giving without guarantee.

Psychologically, humans risk forgetting these truths under the flood of machine imitation. The danger is not that machines surpass humans — but that humans surrender their sacredness.

Case Studies & History

Case Study 1: Art as Resistance
AI generates paintings in milliseconds. Yet Banksy, with one spray can, disrupts the world. Art's power lies not in output but intent.

Case Study 2: Music Beyond Code
Machines can compose symphonies, but they cannot recreate Coltrane's improvisation in a smoky club, born of pain and prayer.

Case Study 3: Ritual and Spirit
AI sermons may comfort, but they lack the trembling voice of a preacher who lived through fire and speaks from scars.

Case Study 4: Death and Grief
AI can mimic voices of the dead, but it cannot sit in silence at a graveside, holding a hand, carrying loss.

Historical Parallel: The Survival of Storytelling

Even under empire, slavery, and oppression, oral traditions survived. Machines cannot replace the stories whispered in kitchens, on porches, around fires.

Corporate vs. Street POV

Corporate: “AI makes us more human.”

Street: “It makes us forget what human is.”

Corporate: “Technology fills the gaps.”

Street: “It widens the wound.”

Corporate: “Machines expand creativity.”

Street: “They copy — they don’t create.”

Corporate: “The human spirit is outdated.”

Street: “It is eternal.”

Parable

Marcus worked in a factory replaced by robots. He felt useless. One night, his daughter woke screaming from a nightmare. He held her, whispered comfort, and sang an off-key lullaby. She fell asleep in his arms.

The robots could work faster. They could assemble cleaner. But they could never hold his child with trembling hands, never give comfort born of love.

Marcus realized: his worth was not in the machine’s measure. It was in the sacred things only he could give.

Real-Life Examples

Indigenous communities keeping sacred ceremonies alive despite digital erasure.

Families gathering for funerals where no algorithm can mediate grief.

Protesters in the streets chanting, singing, crying — AI can record but never replicate the spirit of defiance.

A mother's embrace, a mentor's wisdom, a lover's devotion — all irreplaceable, all unprogrammable.

Chapter Manifesto

We declare: the human is sacred.

We reject the lie that code can capture conscience.
We reject the theft of creativity as if art is data.
We reject the illusion that machines can love.

Our manifesto: the soul is beyond simulation. The sacred human cannot be replaced. We hold this truth as the foundation of survival.

Survival Solutions

Practice humanity daily: Love, create, sacrifice, share — in ways machines cannot.

Protect sacred spaces: Homes, rituals, and communities free from automation.

Elevate human labor: Value caregiving, teaching, mentoring — work that resists automation.

Preserve memory: Oral histories, rituals, and traditions that no algorithm can own.

Rebuild reverence: Teach children that humanity itself is the miracle, not the machine.

Future Scenario

By 2050, machines may perform nearly every economic task. But the survival of humanity will not depend on competing with AI. It will depend on reclaiming what machines cannot touch.

The sacred human will become rebellion: touch in a touchless world, stories in a world of data, sacrifice in a world of profit. Those who remember what cannot be automated will lead the future.

Prophecy Close

Prophecy closes with this: machines may master the field, but they cannot own the spirit. The sacred human endures. And when the world drowns in imitation, it is the human spark that will light the way back.

The machine cannot feel. The machine cannot die. The machine cannot love.

But you can. And that is the revolution.

Chapter 46: Exodus from the Machine — The Birth of Post-AI Communities

Prophecy Opener

They told us there was no way out. They told us the machine was the future, that resistance was futile, that everyone must adapt or perish. But prophecy warns: every empire has an exodus. Just as enslaved people fled plantations, just as oppressed peoples built maroon societies, just as nations broke from kings, so too will humanity birth communities that live beyond the reach of AI.

The prophecy is this: when the machine consumes everything, the survivors will not be those most efficient in code. They will be those who walk away. The future will not belong to the most "advanced" but to the most sovereign. Post-AI communities will rise like new Jerusalems, built not on silicon, but on soil, spirit, and solidarity.

Psychological Breakdown

Why does humanity need exodus to survive?

Dependency as captivity: The machine trains people to believe survival requires its platforms. Exodus breaks the dependency.

Fear of irrelevance: Workers cling to AI jobs, even as those jobs vanish. Exodus means redefining value.

Addiction to convenience: People prefer easy consumption over hard freedom. Exodus demands sacrifice.

Collective amnesia: Many forget how to farm, build, heal, and govern without systems. Exodus re-teaches.

Psychic renewal: Breaking from the machine allows communities to rediscover dignity, purpose, and sacred bonds.

Exodus is not escape. It is rebirth.

Case Studies & History

Case Study 1: Maroon Communities
Escaped slaves built hidden villages in swamps and mountains, thriving outside empires. Sovereignty was survival.

Case Study 2: Kibbutzim in Israel
Collective farms built after colonial upheaval show how intentional community can thrive against hostile odds.

Case Study 3: Amish Resistance
Rejecting certain technologies, Amish communities demonstrate how boundaries preserve identity and independence.

Case Study 4: Zapatista Autonomous Zones
Indigenous rebels in Mexico resisted state and corporate power by building sovereign schools, clinics, and governance.

Historical Parallel: Exodus from Egypt
The Israelites walked out of empire into wilderness. Exodus is always painful, but it births nations.

Corporate vs. Street POV

Corporate: “There is no alternative to AI.”

Street: “Alternatives have always existed — they just require courage.”

Corporate: “Exodus is regression.”

Street: “Exodus is progression — toward sovereignty.”

Corporate: “Only integration ensures survival.”

Street: “Integration ensures captivity.”

Corporate: “The future is centralized.”

Street: “The future is sovereign.”

Parable

A group of workers in 2035 saw their town hollowed out by automation. Factories closed. Schools replaced teachers with screens. Clinics replaced doctors with bots. Families dissolved into endless scrolling.

One night, they gathered in an abandoned church. They swore to build a life without the machine. They pooled money, bought land, planted gardens, raised livestock. They taught children skills the machine could not erase.

Five years later, while nearby towns begged tech corporations for aid, their community thrived. They were poor in dollars but rich in sovereignty. They had built a post-AI tribe.

Real-Life Examples

Off-grid communities in the U.S. and Europe already rejecting digital surveillance.

Indigenous groups reviving ancestral agriculture to resist corporate agribusiness.

Tech workers leaving Silicon Valley to form communes focused on human connection.

Religious sects building intentional villages as sanctuaries from digital overload.

Chapter Manifesto

We declare: the machine is not destiny.

We reject the lie that humanity must surrender to code.

We reject the theft of sovereignty disguised as innovation.

We reject the belief that survival requires captivity.

Our manifesto: exodus is not escape — it is freedom. Post-AI communities will rise not in the image of the machine but in the memory of ancestors, rooted in soil, culture, and sacrifice.

Survival Solutions

Land acquisition: Secure territory where sovereignty can be built beyond corporate reach.

Skill revival: Teach farming, carpentry, medicine, and governance without machines.

Economic independence: Build barter systems, local currencies, and cooperative ownership.

Cultural anchoring: Use rituals, storytelling, and shared meals to bind community.

Defensive networks: Protect communities from infiltration, surveillance, and dependency traps.

Future Scenario

By 2050, humanity may split into two worlds: hyper-integrated machine cities and sovereign post-AI enclaves. The cities will boast convenience but breed despair. The enclaves will struggle but live free.

In these enclaves, children will grow without digital chains. They will know soil, stars, and songs. They will know stories not written by algorithms but by elders. From these seeds, a new civilization may grow.

Prophecy Close

Prophecy closes with this: exodus is always costly. Wilderness is always hard. But captivity is harder. The machine will enslave all who cling to it. Freedom will belong to those who walk away.

Exodus is not the end. It is the beginning. And the post-AI world will be built not by machines, but by the sacred human hand.

Chapter 47: The Algorithmic Empire — When Corporations Become Nations

Prophecy Opener

Once, empires were carved with swords and guarded by armies. Now, they are built with servers and guarded by algorithms. Borders no longer mark power — data does. Parliaments and presidents may still exist, but their reach is weaker than the digital sovereigns who hold the screens, the platforms, and the pipelines of code.

The prophecy is this: the age of nations will end, and the age of algorithmic empires will rise. Corporations will not just influence governments; they will replace them. Laws will be written in terms of service. Rights will be determined by login access. Citizenship will be reduced to user status. Those who cannot comply will be exiled — digitally first, physically later.

Psychological Breakdown

How does the algorithmic empire capture human minds?

Dependency on platforms: People cannot communicate, work, or trade without corporate apps. To lose access is to lose survival.

Normalization of terms: "I agree" buttons teach obedience. People surrender rights with a click.

False choice illusion: Users think they have options, but every platform feeds into the same corporate power web.

Fear of invisibility: To be deleted from platforms feels like social death. This keeps people compliant.

Identity colonization: People no longer see themselves as citizens of nations but as members of corporate ecosystems (Apple, Google, Meta).

Psychologically, the empire doesn't need armies. It needs loyalty to convenience.

Case Studies & History

Case Study 1: East India Company
The first corporate empire conquered nations and ran them for profit. Today's platforms mirror its model.

Case Study 2: Facebook & Myanmar
Social media manipulated an entire nation's politics, fueling genocide through algorithmic propaganda.

Case Study 3: Amazon's Marketplace
Cities now depend on Amazon distribution the way colonies once depended on imperial ports.

Case Study 4: China's Social Credit System
An example of digital governance where freedom is tied to algorithmic scoring.

History repeats — the sword becomes the server.

Corporate vs. Street POV

Corporate: "We provide services that governments can't."

Street: "You replaced government with monopoly."

Corporate: “We empower users.”

Street: “You enslave users with dependency.”

Corporate: “Regulation will keep us in check.”

Street: “You write the regulations yourselves.”

Corporate: “We build community.”

Street: “You sell community as product.”

Parable

In 2040, a small town lost its government funding. Its schools, utilities, and even police force collapsed. A major corporation stepped in: they provided AI teachers, drone delivery, and even patrol robots. The town signed a contract.

At first, life seemed better. But every service came with rules. Children could not attend class unless parents uploaded biometric data. Drones refused to deliver to households that failed monthly subscription payments. Patrol bots enforced “terms of service” instead of laws.

One family rebelled — they refused to surrender their privacy. Overnight, their accounts were deleted. No access to groceries, schools, or healthcare. They had not broken the law. They had broken the algorithm.

Real-Life Examples

Cities already negotiating with Amazon and Google for infrastructure.

Schools outsourcing curriculum to tech firms.

Banks using corporate data scores to approve or deny loans.

Politicians taking orders from platform lobbyists.

“Shadow governance” where corporate contracts override constitutional rights.

Chapter Manifesto

We declare: corporations are not nations, and algorithms are not laws.

We reject the captivity of terms of service masquerading as constitutions.
We reject the surrender of human rights to digital monopolies.
We reject the empire that enslaves with convenience instead of chains.

Our manifesto: nations belong to people, not to platforms.

Survival Solutions

Digital sovereignty: Build independent networks, platforms, and tools outside corporate control.

Local governance: Strengthen councils, co-ops, and communities to resist outsourcing democracy.

Collective bargaining with platforms: Communities demanding contracts, not just individuals clicking “I agree.”

Diversification of dependencies: Never let one corporation own food, water, communication, and medicine.

Education: Teach youth to see platforms as tools, not as gods.

Future Scenario

By 2050, algorithmic empires will openly govern. "Countries" may still exist, but their power will be symbolic. The real power will be with corporations who control:

The platforms where citizens work.

The apps where citizens socialize.

The currencies citizens spend.

The surveillance systems citizens live under.

A rebellion will rise — not of armies, but of sovereign communities that refuse to click "I agree." They will build parallel economies, encrypted systems, and sovereign villages.

The question will not be "Are you free?" but "Which empire do you serve — the nation or the algorithm?"

Prophecy Close

The prophecy closes with this: the greatest empire in history will not fly a flag. It will fly a logo. And the greatest rebellion in history will not be fought on battlefields. It will be fought in communities that choose sovereignty over convenience.

Final Manifesto: The Last Five Years

We declare: labor as we knew it is gone. The system will not save you. Politicians cannot protect you. Corporations will not free you. The machine age is not coming — it is here.

We reject the myth that hard work guarantees safety. We reject the leash disguised as a paycheck, the prison disguised as a mortgage, the chain disguised as a diploma. We reject the illusion that coding, hustling, or overworking will save us when the very system profits from exhaustion.

We declare: survival in the age of AI is not about jobs — it is about ownership. Ownership of land. Ownership of tools. Ownership of ideas. Ownership of community.

We affirm: the last wealth that cannot be automated is human. Our creativity, our spirit, our communities, our refusal to surrender sovereignty — these are the final currencies.

We warn: the window is closing. In five years, the gap will widen beyond repair. The middle will vanish, the poor will expand, and the AI lords will own the gates. Those who wait will be locked out. Those who build will endure.

We commit: to group economics, to sovereign communities, to teaching our children not to serve algorithms but to master them. To planting food, not just consuming brands. To creating art, not just scrolling feeds. To building tribes, not just profiles.

Our manifesto is simple: own or be owned. Build or be buried. Unite or be erased.

The prophecy closes with this: in the end, freedom will not be given. It must be built. And those who build now — in these last years of labor — will inherit the future.

About the Author

Patrice Shabazz is a son of North Carolina — raised by hardship, hardened by experience, and healed through truth. A sharp voice forged in poverty, he writes to expose the systems that keep everyday people buried under debt, silence, and struggle. His words don't just teach — they testify.

Patrice's mission reaches beyond the page. He is actively working to build a self-sustainable community rooted in group economics, accountability, and liberation. Through books, outreach, and strategic action, he's not just telling stories — he's blueprinting solutions.

If you are a like-minded individual, a builder, a visionary, or simply someone curious about how we rise together, reach out: patriceshabazz39@gmail.com

———

"A lone runner may reach the hill first — but a village crosses mountains."

— Patrice Shabazz

Led by Patrice Shabazz | Founder, Exclusive Heights

We're building more than a neighborhood — we're building a future.

The Vision

Imagine 300–500 acres of land, powered by solar, growing our own food, raising livestock, creating jobs, and raising children in a safe, educated, self-governed environment.

This isn't a dream. This is a blueprint.

We're forming a 1,000-person self-sustainable Black-led community rooted in:

- Group economics
- Cooperative living
- Clean food, clean water, clean energy
- Vocational training & land-based education
- Mental, physical, and financial healing

The Math & Mission

- Goal: $12,000 per person x 1,000 = $12 million
- Covers: Land (300–500 acres), infrastructure, housing, farming, solar, schools, tradespaces, and startup capital for community-owned businesses.

Every dollar goes into ownership, food security, and generational wealth — not rent.

Who We're Looking For

We're recruiting:

- Skilled tradespeople: Electricians, Plumbers, Builders, Farmers, HVAC, Welders
- Educators & Mentors: Teachers, Counselors, Homeschoolers, Youth Leaders
- Medical & Holistic Health: Nurses, CNAs, Herbalists, Wellness Coaches
- Tech & Media: Web Designers, Editors, Content Creators
- General Builders: Visionaries willing to work, grow, and invest in change

---

Why Join?

- Be part of a legacy project
- Live and work with purpose
- Help build Black independence
- Escape survival mode and enter sustainability
- Your name will be on the foundation of a new nation within a nation

---

Support & Donate

Help fund the first phase:

- [GoFundMe gofund.me/637427e2]
- Cash App: $ExclusiveHeights

Every donation brings us one step closer to land, infrastructure, and freedom.

Get Involved

Contact: patriceshabazz39@gmail.com
Based in North Carolina — open to national collaboration

———

"A system built to bury us… won't survive the ones who plant back."
— Patrice Shabazz

Made in the USA
Monee, IL
05 November 2026

68020971R00152